MW01234893

Praise for The Millionaire & ME

"Every year I try to meet with my new teachers to instill the power of compounding interest and the importance of beginning this process during year one. The Millionaire & ME takes the financial planning conversation to the next level. I have purchased a copy for every new teacher as well as buying several additional copies for our professional library. If you are a teacher who wants to retire comfortably, this book is a must!"

Thomas Trippany, EdS – Principal

"Dr. Frandsen has written a must-read motivator for anyone considering the education profession . . . Read this book – and learn how to make a difference in the world while also making a difference in your wallet."

Lora Knudsen, MSW– Teacher and School Counselor

"As a kid I always thought about being a teacher but was always deterred when people said they didn't make enough money. The Millionaire & ME helped me understand how I can make a comfortable lifestyle and career out of teaching. Even if I don't choose education as a career I know the wisdom provided in these pages will be a help in any field!"

Zabel Human – College student and prospective teacher

"Dr. Frandsen has taken his accumulated knowledge and tailor-fit his expertise for the most taken-for-granted profession in our country. The levers identified in The Millionaire and Me are key movements toward a successful retirement for any educator. What a great resource in a much needed time!"

Lori Jackson – author of Practicing Progress and Hoping for Happy; owner of choosingwisdom.com

The Millionaire & ME

A Teacher's Guide to Becoming a Millionaire

Dr Steve Frandsen

The Millionaire & ME

A Teacher's Guide to Becoming a Millionaire

Illustrations by Ty Frandsen

Jacket art by Brian Frandsen

Photo on back cover by Stefani Frandsen

Edited by Aubrey Parry ravishingrevisions@gmail.com

Printed in the United States of America

First Printing: April 2021

ISBN: 9798730948617

Dedicated to those who endeavor to teach!

Contents

Disclaimer

I'm just a guy with more than twenty years working in the K-12 and university settings with a high interest in personal finance. Beginning in college, I made it a habit to read books, articles, and blogs about personal finance and investing. I listen to podcasts and radio shows, and I love talking to anyone with an expertise in finance. I have also noticed over the years that there are many educators who are able to retire very wealthy. I have talked to them and have learned about what they did right and what mistakes they made along their path. The strategies in this book are a culmination of that research and of those conversations. The chapters include dollar amounts that were calculated using simple retirement and investment calculators available online. These are estimates and are shared to illustrate what is possible, individual results will vary. I am not a financial expert nor a financial advisor.

Introduction

So, you're an educator, or you're interested in becoming one. Congratulations on a great career choice! I, along with many others, happen to think that a career in education is one of the most rewarding professions in the world. You get to impact future generations. You get to give back to the community. You get to share your passion of literature, math, art, or whatever your passion may be with the youth of the world, and you get to help them find their passions. Another awesome part of being an educator is that you get to become a millionaire too! Wait . . . what?

You've probably heard all the former reasons to get into teaching, but you probably haven't heard the latter reason! I know I didn't. As a matter of fact, my mother tried to talk me out of going into teaching because I wouldn't make any money. When I graduated college and started teaching, many of my friends from college would make fun of me and my teacher's salary as they were off trying to make money in business, sales, and real estate. They were more than happy to tell me about how much they were making or how much they could potentially make if they made certain quotas or goals. The good-natured ribbing of my fun-loving friends began to make me wonder if maybe I *had* chosen the wrong profession. Not only did I have a healthy case of FOMO (fear of missing out) but I began to feel a little foolish that they could make all of this money and that maybe I was falling behind. I even began to fear that I wasn't going to make enough to provide for my family on what I thought at the time was modest income.

When I shared with my wife that I was thinking of leaving the profession for greener pastures (pun intended), she set me straight and said, "I married a teacher. You are a teacher!" Hearing her support of my career choice eased some of my fears. After all, we were both high school Spanish teachers at the time, and we loved having the same schedule and interests. Our life was simple and lovely. But I knew that we both wanted to have a large family, and I knew that a large family would eventually put enormous stress on the budget. Thus began our journey of figuring out how to make the honorable and noble profession of teaching make us some money.

Now, into my third decade in the profession, I have seen many people enter the profession right out of college, young, wide-eyed, and ready to change the world. I have also seen people come to the profession later in life after realizing that they missed their true calling. Many times, they have told me that they knew all along that they were supposed to teach but they resisted because they thought they could make more money in the private sector. In the end, they came back to where they knew they should have started all along. Unfortunately, I have also seen some colleagues succumb to the temptation I had early in my career to leave the profession in search for something different.

With the people who remain in the profession and make it to retirement, one thing I've noticed time and time again is that there are so many people who not only make the noble profession of teaching work for their families but they retire like millionaires, and in many cases, they retire *as* millionaires!

I'm not the only one who has taken notice of this trend. In 1996, Dr. Thomas Stanley and Dr. William Danko wrote the book, *The Millionaire Next Door: The Surprising Secrets of America's Wealthy,* which shared their research on millionaires. They found that teachers were often part of a group they referred to as Prodigious Accumulators of Wealth, or PAWs. This group of PAWs resulted in a surprising number of teachers who were in the unconventional and unexpected group of millionaires who live next door.[1] In the book *Everyday Millionaires: How Ordinary People Built Extraordinary Wealth—and How You Can Too*, Chris Hogan shares the results of his research where he surveyed over 10,000 millionaires. One surprising find for Chris was that teaching was the third most common profession of the everyday millionaires he surveyed.[2] That means that for the past twenty-five years, researchers have been surprised to see *teaching* as a recurring profession among the ranks of millionaires in this country!

> **Top three occupations of everyday millionaires are:**
>
> **1. Engineer**
>
> **2. Accountant**
>
> **3. Teacher**
>
> **- Chris Hogan (emphasis added)**

The Purpose

The purpose of this book is to encourage the recruitment and retention of teachers to the profession. A lot has been written about the teacher shortage in America and the difficulties schools have with retaining teachers after they begin. Depending on the study, you can see that as many as 50% of the teachers that begin teaching leave the profession within five years.[3] Many articles have been written that address ways to remedy that phenomenon. This book will focus on one aspect of why anyone should enter the profession and stay in the teaching game that other articles largely ignore: the money. A commonly held misperception is that teachers do not go into teaching for the money. It may even strike you as counterintuitive when I make the claim that if you stay in teaching; not only can you retire relatively young but you can also retire rich!

Another purpose of this book is to serve as an introduction to some tools, referred to as levers, that are available to teachers. Understanding the basics of these levers can motivate you to study each lever in depth in order to take advantage of them in your personal career and financial journey. The discussions of each lever in this book are broad in nature and are in no way exhaustive. I'm merely trying to bring each of the levers to your awareness and encourage you to research them further to see how you can leverage them to your advantage. These levers are not complex, but when understood and used consistently over a teaching career, they give you the formula to become a millionaire or its equivalent.

What do you want?

Before we begin discussing the specific levers that we can use to retire a millionaire or its equivalent, I would like you to ask yourself a few questions: Is this a goal you are interested in making? Is this a worthwhile goal for you and your family? Are you interested in achieving excellence in this regard?

If you answered with an enthusiastic "yes!" to these questions, I would ask you to commit to developing the habits we'll discuss that will allow you to use the levers discussed in this book. Will Durant, author of *The Story of Philosophy: The Lives and Opinions of the Worlds Greatest Philosophers from Plato to John Dewey*, once said the following, which is often misattributed to Aristotle: "We are what we repeatedly do. Excellence, then, is not an act, but a habit." In this book, we're going to discuss principles that, if done habitually, will produce excellence in your career and in your life.

> **We are what we repeatedly do. Excellence, then, is not an act, but a habit.**
>
> **- Will Durant**

In his book, *Seven Habits of Highly Effective People: Powerful Lessons in Personal Change*, Stephen R. Covey articulates very important habits that, when developed and applied consistently, increase an individual's effectiveness. One habit he shares is to "begin with the end in mind." For the purposes of this book, I want you to consider "the end" to mean the end of your teaching career and what your financial situation will be at that time. What is the financial end that you desire for you and your family? Do you want to end your teaching career as a millionaire? If so, how are you going to make that happen?

> **All things are created twice.**
>
> **- Stephen R. Covey**

Covey shares that "all things are created twice." The first creation is mental, and the second creation is physical.[4] These creations can be by design or by default. You can actively participate in designing the creation mentally and physically, or you can let things happen and see how they turn out.

In this book, I ask you to commit to actively participating in the creation of becoming a millionaire through your career in the teaching profession. That is the financial end that I want you to begin with as you approach your careers.

Prerequisites

Since we're talking about something as impressive as becoming a millionaire, let's discuss a few prerequisites that you'll need if you're going to attempt to achieve something as great as having a million dollars or its equivalent for retirement whether you accomplish this feat through teaching or through another career.

First Prerequisite—Hard Work

Margaret Thatcher once said, "I do not know anyone who has got to the top without hard work. That is the recipe! It will not always get you to the top but should get you pretty near." Teaching is a tough profession, and there is no substitute for hard work! But if you're going to be a millionaire, teaching is a vehicle that can take you there as long as you work hard for it. You have to be willing to do the things we discuss in this book even if they may disrupt current habits.

Second prerequisite—Discipline

I've never heard of any individual or team winning a championship, accomplishing a difficult goal, or achieving excellence without discipline. Discipline is pushing yourself to do things that you may not want to do but that you know will benefit you in the long run. You do not stumble upon being a millionaire in teaching. As Stephen Covey said, you create it twice. You make a plan and then you make it happen through discipline.

Third prerequisite—Persistence

Most people are familiar with the fable of the tortoise and the hare. It's a powerful lesson of persistence! The tortoise was persistent. He stayed the course and stayed focused on winning the race while the hare was much faster but was easily distracted. The rabbit's inconsistent effort ultimately made him lose the race. It may sound cliché, but slow and steady does win the race.

Undoubtedly, you'll make some mistakes along the way. There will be days where you'll want to quit the plan or even the job. You will have to persist! I can't tell you how many smart, dedicated, and talented teachers I've worked with who left the profession to find their pot of gold somewhere else only to return a few years later having rediscovered that teaching is an amazing gig with significant financial benefits.

I truly hope you ponder these prerequisites and commit to them. You will need them throughout your teaching career and financial journey.

Levers

You may have noticed I've been using the concept of a lever in reference to how you can become a millionaire. Every book I've read on retirement or on how to become a millionaire refers to the power of the lever, as will this book.

Hopefully, at this point, you've envisioned a lever and fulcrum and you think back to the lessons in grade school about simple machines.

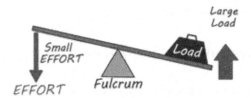

We know that we can exert a small force downward to move a heavy load upward, and depending on the length of the lever and the position of the fulcrum, the results can be dramatic—so much so that the Greek mathematician Archimedes said:

"Give me a lever long enough and I can move the world."

We're not trying to move the world, but with these levers, we *can* become millionaires.

In financial circles, the concept of leverage is everywhere. How can anyone invest a little money, time, or effort to achieve great gains or results? There are books on how you can use the levers of the stock markets, commodities, real estate, bitcoin, etc. This book will focus on five levers educators can employ to lift their financial status to that of a millionaire or its equivalent if they stick to the prerequisites of hard work, discipline, and persistence.

In some instances, the levers are highlighted in this book are similar to the concepts you may see in other books, but in other instances, I'll go over important and powerful levers that are available only to teachers.

The levers we will look at are as follows:

Lever 1—Maximize Your Retirement Plan (Pension)

This lever is less common outside of the teaching profession. We'll discuss how retirement plans work and look at real examples that show how you can retire very close to a millionaire with this lever alone.

Lever 2—Make This Profession Pay You

The compensation schedule for teachers is fixed and predictable. We'll discuss the rules of the compensation game and how you can use them to maximize your earning potential in teaching.

Lever 3—Tell Your Money What to Do

Few people accidentally end up with money in their accounts, but many accidentally end up broke. We'll discuss the components of a successful budgeting plan and make the case of why you should consistently execute that plan.

Lever 4—Put Your Money to Work

If you're going to retire a **M**illionaire **E**quivalent (**ME**), you need to consistently invest the money you set aside in your budget. We'll discuss readily available options for teachers that can ensure you retire a **M**illionaire **E**quivalent or even a **T**rue **M**illionaire (**TM**).

Lever 5—Expand Your Options

We'll discuss ways to maximize your assets in order to retire a **T**rue **M**illionaire.

Defining Terms

In addition to the prerequisites and the reminder of the great load we can lift with levers, I'll define what I mean when I say you can retire a millionaire. By utilizing the five levers and through consistent hard work, discipline, and persistence, anyone can work their way into the classifications of a **Millionaire Equivalent** or a **True Millionaire** when they retire.

True Millionaire (TM) vs. Millionaire Equivalent (ME)

What is a millionaire? Is it someone who has a million-dollar home? Is it someone who has a personal residence, a lake house, and cars that combined are valued at a million dollars? Or is it someone who has a million dollars in assets?

In his book, *Rich Dad Poor Dad: What the Rich Teach Their Kids about Money—That the Poor and Middle Class Do Not,* Robert T. Kyosaki gives a simple definition of assets and liabilities that we'll use throughout this book:

Assets put money into your pocket.

Liabilities take money out of your pocket.[5]

By these definitions, your cars, personal homes, vacation homes, clothes, etc. would be considered **liabilities**. They consistently take money out of your pocket.

Individual Retirement Accounts (IRAs), savings accounts, rental properties, or any other properties that create money would be considered **assets**. These things consistently put money into your pocket.

Introduction

Throughout this book you'll see the two acronyms **TM** and **ME**. When I refer to a **TM** (**T**rue **M**illionaire), I'm referring to someone who accumulates one or more retirement accounts whose total value is equal to or greater than $1,000,000. I'm not referring to someone with a net worth (assets and liabilities) that equals $1,000,000.

What I mean by becoming a **M**illionaire **E**quivalent or **ME** is that by earning the equivalent of a **T**rue **M**illionaire (**TM**) every year throughout your retirement, you are essentially the equivalent of a millionaire.

In this book we'll focus on **T**rue **M**illionaires having a million dollars in an IRA rather than having a million dollars in assets and liabilities because an IRA will produce a passive income every year that will be enough to live comfortably throughout retirement. If you have an IRA worth a million dollars, that IRA will produce money every year. Whereas having a home worth $500,000, cars worth $100,000, a bank account with $100,000 and an IRA worth $300,000 would make you worth $1,000,000 and technically a millionaire, but your possessions would not produce the kind of money through retirement that having an IRA worth $1,000,000 would produce.

An IRA with $1,000,000 earning 8% interest will produce $80,000 pre-tax every year throughout retirement. Depending on how the markets go, some years it will produce more and some years it will produce less. On average, an 8% return is a modest growth prediction.

True Millionaire (TM)—A **T**rue **M**illionaire has a minimum of $1,000,000 in one or more IRAs.

For example, Lawrence is a **TM** because he has $1,000,000 in a mutual fund that earns 8% a year. This means he earns $80,000 a year for the rest of his life.

If a **TM** will earn $80,000 a year from a $1,000,000 IRA that earns 8% a year, someone who falls in the category of a **ME** would then earn a minimum of $80,000 a year in retirement even if he or she does not have $1,000,000 in his or her IRA. Teachers can achieve this level of payout with their full retirement plan coupled with personal IRA or other assets. These two combined can kick out the **equivalent** of a **TM**'s fully funded $1,000,000 IRA.

Millionaire Equivalent (ME)—A teacher's retirement plan yearly payout + his or her personal IRA yearly payout = the equivalent of the payout of $1,000,000 invested in an IRA.

For example, Silvia is a **ME** because she has a state retirement plan that produces $60,000 a year in addition to $250,000 in a personal IRA that produces $20,000 a year. Both these assets together earn the equivalent of the **TM**'s yearly payout.

When we approach our retirement with this in mind, the possibility of retiring a **ME** is easily attainable to anyone who employs the three prerequisites that we talked about (hard work, discipline, and persistence).

On a personal note . . .

At the end of each chapter, I'll share some personal information about my family's journey. The reason I share these vignettes is not to brag in any way but is to personalize the concepts I've shared and to illustrate how I've successfully used them or neglected them at different moments of my life and career. You'll see that some of my choices are not brag worthy at all; maybe they can serve as a voice of warning.

I'm the fifth of seven children. My sister is the oldest child followed by six boys. Growing up there wasn't a lot of money around the house. In fact, we qualified for Free Lunches at school. Maybe that is why I have had such an interest in finances for most of my adult life. Scarcity at a young age can have that effect on you. We lived in a modest home, and what we lacked in financial resources, we made up for with lots of love and support. The house only had three bedrooms, an unfinished storage area that we used as a fourth bedroom, and one bathroom. One bedroom was for my parents, and with there being only one girl, my sister got her own room. That left six boys to share the remaining room and the unfinished storage area. And with seven kids and two parents, you can imagine the line we had for that one bathroom. We shared everything! We did not live in the best area or go to the best high school in town, but I absolutely loved every part of my childhood.

I graduated college with a bachelor's degree in Spanish teaching at the age of twenty-six with $13,000 in student loans and consumer debt. I packed everything I owned in a 1990 blue Geo Metro that didn't have air-conditioning and moved to Georgia to begin my teaching career. I got married at twenty-eight, and my sweet wife and I had five children. My wife taught for five years before making the decision to stay home with the kids when our second child was born. She was out of the workplace for fifteen years while doing some of the most important work on the planet—raising the sweetest, most important children ever to be made! That means we spent fifteen years raising a family of seven on one educator's income.

In many ways, when my wife and I first began teaching, we were typical beginning teachers starting our careers with a good chunk of debt and plans to start a family. As time has progressed, I've noticed that we've made financial sacrifices that shouldn't be atypical but that have put us on track to retire well beyond a **ME.** We plan to achieve the status of a **TM.** Your situation may be similar in that you begin your career in debt or that you find yourself in a single income scenario or both. I share this information to say that if my wife and I can do it, anyone can!

Chapter 1

Lever 1—Maximize your Retirement Plan (Pension)

D o you remember how my friends made fun of my modest teacher salary? They were merciless in their taunting about how much money they were making and were going to make. Well, when I tell them about my retirement plan and the benefits it will kick out and when I tell them I can start receiving those benefits when I'm at the ripe young age of fifty-four, let me tell you, they don't make fun of me anymore! They are green with envy! There is nothing out there in the market like the retirement plans or pensions most states provide educators.

The biggest lever an educator has to retire as a millionaire is a full retirement benefit. If you're able to earn a full retirement benefit, you're already well on your way to be a **ME** (**M**illionaire Equivalent) and will probably be able to achieve the status of **TM** (**T**rue **M**illionaire) before it's all said and done!

Let me define what I mean by a full retirement benefit or a full pension. I'm referring to a full pension plan that you can earn when you stay in the profession for twenty-five years or more depending on the state.

Many people enter the profession at different times in their life. In fact, the average age of someone entering the profession is twenty-nine.[6] I entered the profession at twenty-six, just below the national average. That means that in my state, I can retire with a full retirement benefit at age fifty-six, or fifty-four if I choose to apply my accrued sick leave. That's a full decade before my mocking friends will even start thinking about being able to retire! If you're fortunate enough to enter the profession earlier, you may be able to retire much earlier. Think about it: if you were able to graduate high school at age eighteen and finish college in four years, then you would begin teaching at age twenty-two. If you taught for twenty-eight years and accrued two years of sick leave during that time, you would be able to retire at age fifty! That's crazy talk! That's unheard of!

Each state has its own retirement plan and different rules that govern the plan, so it's imperative that you find out the rules of your state as soon as you can to leverage the plan to your benefit as much as possible. Some state retirement plans are in good standing, while others are underfunded. Often, as the state makes changes to its plan, the state will either grandfather you in with the plan that you started your career with, or they will make wholesale changes. Make sure you're aware of your state's plan so you can adjust your plans as the rules of the game may change. As I said, this is the biggest lever available to you in the teaching profession, so it's in your best interest to pay attention to it.

To give you an idea of the potential amounts you can earn from a pension, in Georgia, each teacher contributes 6% of their salary every month into the state's TRS (Teacher Retirement System). In return, you earn 2% of your highest two-year average salary for every year that you work up to forty years. So that means a teacher could earn up to 80% of their highest two-year average salary every year for the rest of his or her life if he or she worked forty years.[7]

The key for you to become a **ME** and eventually a **TM** is to know how much your benefits will be and see if there's a gap between your teacher's retirement payout and the **TM** payout of $80,000 a year.

Each state has different payout options. You could take out a larger amount that ends when you pass away, or you could take out less each year and have that benefit continue for your beneficiary or beneficiaries until they pass away. For our purposes, let's look at three examples that take out the full amount each year until they pass away to illustrate just how powerful these full benefit plans can be.

Example 1 (low)

Doug began teaching at age twenty-nine and is now ready to retire at age fifty-nine. Doug worked in a number of schools in the state for thirty years, but he didn't earn any additional degrees. At the time of his retirement, the district he worked for had a pay scale with a maximum salary of $71,000 for a teacher with a bachelor's degree after he or she has taught for twenty-eight years. That means that Doug would have earned $71,000 for his twenty-ninth and thirtieth years of service. Doug qualified for 2% for each year he worked, for a total of 60% of the average of his highest two years' salaries. The average of his highest two years' salaries was $71,000. The result was that Doug earned a full retirement that will return **$42,600 a year** for the rest of his life! Even with this handsome payout, we still see that Doug has not yet achieved the status of a **ME**. He has a gap of $37,400 a year to reach the $80,000 a year that a **TM** earns. We'll call that a **TM gap** of $37,400.

Doug's scenario:

2% per year X 30 years= 60%

Average of Highest 2 years X 60%

$71,000 X 0.60 = $42,600

TM gap: $80,000 - $42,600 = $37,400

Doug is well on his way to become a **ME**, but he still has work to do. In order for Doug to become a **ME**, he would have needed to utilize the other levers in this book, which we'll discuss in later chapters.

Example 2 (Middle)

Katrina began teaching at age twenty-five and chose to retire at age fifty-seven. Katrina earned a master's degree ten years after starting teaching and has worked in the same school district for her entire career. The salary scale for her school district has a maximum salary of $81,000 after twenty-eight years of teaching. Katrina's retirement would pay out 2% a year for her thirty-two years of service for a total of 64% of the average of her highest two years' salary. The result was that Katrina earned a full retirement with a payout of **$51,840 a year** for the rest of her life!

Katrina's Scenario:

2% per year X 32 years= 64%

Average of Highest 2 years X 64%

$81,000 X .64 = $51,840

TM gap: $80,000 - $51,840 = $28,160

You can see that Katrina was closer to the goal of the **TM**'s $80,000 yearly payout throughout retirement than Doug was, but she still wasn't quite there. Like Doug, Katrina would have needed to employ the other levers outlined in later chapters if she was to become a **ME** and potentially a **TM** herself.

Example 3 (high)

Suzanne began teaching at age twenty-two and chose to retire at age fifty-five. Suzanne continued her education while teaching and earned a doctorate degree. Dr. Suzanne taught in various schools in the state during her career. Her pay scale had a maximum salary of $100,000 a year for a teacher with a doctorate degree who has taught for at least twenty-eight years. She would earn 2% a year for each of the thirty-three years she taught. That means that she would receive a full retirement payout of 66% of the average of her highest two years' salaries, or **$66,000 a year** for the rest of her life! Keep in mind that Dr. Suzanne would have retired a full decade before her peers typically would retire! She was only fifty-five years old!

Dr. Suzanne's scenario:

2% per year X 33 years= 66%

Average of Highest 2 years X 66%

$100,000 X .66 = $66,000

TM gap: $80,000 - $66,000 = $14,000

Dr. Suzanne would be very close to achieving **TM** status without any additional personal IRA payouts. She would definitely be able to become a **ME** and would be well on her way to becoming a **TM**! She would still need to utilize the remaining levers of this book to achieve this goal, but she would be in excellent shape.

One thing I'd like to point out is that these salaries are based on a 2020 salary schedule of a county in metro Atlanta, Georgia. Most of you will likely retire years from now, and these numbers will be higher. In addition, the calculation is based on the average of the highest two years of your salary. For most people, those two years are the last two years of their career.

Sick days

How can you get even better results than these examples? In Georgia, you can accrue up to two years of sick leave. How could that impact the numbers shared? Well, if you accrue one- or two-years' worth of sick leave, then you could retire that much time before the thirty-year requirement. If you choose to work the full thirty years, then the accrued sick time would be added to the thirty years. This would give you a total of thirty-two years in the calculation even though you only worked for thirty! That's real time or money, whichever suits your circumstance best. That's a real incentive to avoid taking unnecessary mental health days or to schedule annual doctor visits during non-school times. With this in mind, let's look at what would happen to our overachiever Dr. Suzanne's scenario if she had saved two years' worth of sick leave in addition to working thirty-three years with a doctorate degree.

Dr. Suzanne's scenario with 2 years of sick time accrued:

33 years worked + 2 years of accrued sick time = 35

2% per year X 35 years = 70%

Lever 1—Maximize your Retirement Plan (Pension)

Average of Highest 2 years X 70%

$100,000 X .70 = $70,000

TM gap: $80,000 - $70,000 = $10,000

Dr. Suzanne would receive $4,000 dollars more a year for the rest of her life if she was able to accrue the equivalent of two years' worth of sick leave over her thirty-three-year teaching career. Remember, Dr. Suzanne retired at the young age of fifty-five, a full ten years ahead of her peers. If Dr. Suzanne lived to the age of ninety, that means she would earn $4,000 extra a year for thirty-five years! That's an additional $140,000 she would receive as a result of her hard work, discipline, and persistence.

Using our **TM** benchmark of $80,000 a year in retirement, we can see that Dr. Suzanne would be well on her way of achieving the **ME** status with just the first lever! She only needs to make $10,000 more each year with the other levers.

Another amazing aspect of most teacher retirements is that they include an inflation adjustment or COLA (Cost of Living Adjustment). The state of Georgia currently gives a 1.5% COLA to retirees every 6 months (3% annually). That means these numbers should keep up with inflation throughout retirement.

With these examples, I attempted to illustrate a few possible outcomes at retirement for teachers who earn a full retirement. We'll discuss in detail more ways to maximize your income as a teacher in chapter three. Each time we increase our salary as a teacher, we increase the amount we'll get during every year of retirement.

Another important factor I would like to point out is that the figures I have shared are based off a single income. I have done this on purpose; I want to illustrate that this can be done on one income. If you are a single parent or you have a spouse who is not working or is unable to work, you can do this! Teaching provides this huge lever of a pension! If you're in a situation where there *is* another income, then it will just be easier to leverage the personal IRA lever to close the gap with a **TM**. In many cases, teachers are married to other teachers. If that's the case, then you have *two* retirement plans, which will greatly aid in achieving a **ME** and eventually a **TM** status.

I tell teachers all the time that if they use the right levers, the older version of themselves will be very pleased that the younger version of themselves worked and persisted in the profession of teaching!

The older version of you will be very pleased with the younger version of you!

Threats to the effectiveness of this lever

As with any plan, life may happen and exert its will upon you, which can force you to make adjustments to your plan. In most cases, life doesn't ask for your permission, and certain things may be out of your control. But when you have a good plan and a good understanding of all the levers, you can make adjustments to how much weight you put on one lever when you're not able to put as much weight on another lever. And if you notice one of the levers is not producing what you would like it to produce, you can always adjust to put more weight on more productive levers or to make that lever produce more!

Here are a few of the factors or threats that may impact the amount of money the lever of your retirement plan can earn:

Moving from state to state

In the United States of America, we are a mobile society, and sometimes people need to move from state to state one or more times during the thirty-year span of their career. Depending on the frequency of your moves, this could make it difficult to become fully vested in the state's retirement plan where you finally settle down. The good news is that you can often work with the retirement system from one state to transfer your years equivalent to the new state's plan. It's a bit of a process, but I've had many colleagues get their years back from other states and earn their full retirement benefits. This becomes more problematic if you move multiple times and don't become fully vested in each state before you settle down in one area long enough.

Entering the profession after age thirty

This isn't a huge problem; you just need to know that entering the profession later may make it more difficult to achieve the numbers that were shared in this chapter. Depending on the age you began working and the rules of your state, you'll probably need to work until the age of sixty or later, or you may not earn the full retirement percentage. The state of Georgia's formula is 2% for every year worked. This could mean that you may need to work longer to earn the 60%, or you may need to settle for a smaller final percentage if you would rather retire at sixty years old.

Leaving and re-entering the profession

I've mentioned before that after five years in the profession, some-where between 17% to 50% of teachers have already decided to leave. The reasons for leaving the profession can be as simple as changing states in the middle of the year or someone deciding to stay at home to raise young children for a time. Or the reasons could be more complicated such as not feeling supported by administration, parents, or the community. Whatever the reasons teachers leave, many return after a while and finish their career in the teaching profession. This break in teaching could affect the numbers shared in the examples above. Again, this is not a big deal. Just know that you'll need to be aware of the new projected payout and then make the necessary adjustments to the other levers to make up the **TM gap** and ensure that you achieve **ME** status.

The state adjusting the retirement formula

Depending on the financial health of your state's retirement sys-tem, the state may adjust the benefits package. In most cases, these adjustments aren't in your favor. Sometimes these changes don't affect people already in the profession as they may be able to grandfa-ther the benefits package. Other times, these changes can alter how much your retirement plan lever will produce and can make it so you need to adjust the other levers to make sure you're a **ME** at the time of your retirement.

Example

Luis worked in the private sector for years until he realized it wasn't as fulfilling nor as engaging as he had hoped. He decided to follow that calling to teach and entered the profession at age forty with a bachelor's degree and a provisional certificate. After a bumpy start, he worked for twenty years as a teacher and coach before he was ready to retire. At age sixty, he decided it was time to retire. The average of his last two years teaching was $63,000.

Luis's scenario:

2% per year X 20 years = 40%

Average of Highest 2 years X 40%

$63,000 X .40 = $25,200

TM gap: $80,000 - $25,000 = $55,000

Because of the effects of the threat to this lever, Luis had fewer years in the profession. You can see that Luis's payout is less than the previously shared, fully funded scenarios. This is not an insurmountable obstacle for Luis; it simply means he would need to put more focus on the other levers to ensure he could make up the **TM gap** and retire a **ME**.

Remember, to become a **ME,** you need your Retirement Plan and your personal IRA payouts to be the equivalent of what a millionaire's IRA would produce. So there's still a lot Luis could do to make sure he becomes a **ME** by the age of sixty! Even with his shortened teaching career, he can attain **ME** status five years earlier than people in other professions can!

Estimate Your Own Retirement Payout

Now that we are aware of the threats to this lever, now would be a good time for you to estimate how much you'll get in your retirement based on your unique situation. In Georgia, I can access my

Teacher's Retirement System (TRS) website and use a retirement estimate calculator, which gives me a good idea of how much I'll receive throughout retirement. If your state doesn't provide a tool like this, you can contact your district to see if there's a retirement office that can give you personalized information. By calculating your estimate, you can see how much of a **TM gap** you'll have, which can help you stay focused on your goal.

The Georgia TRS calculator uses the following information to provide an estimated monthly payout. Go ahead and write your estimate personal information in the spaces provided to help you visualize your retirement.

Estimated days of accrued sick leave at retirement: _____

Estimated years of service at retirement: _____

Estimated salary at retirement: _____

Estimated payout from your Retirement Plan:
$_____ per year

Your personal **TM gap** is **$80,000** – (<u>The estimated payout above</u>) = $_____

Napoleon Hill, in his book *Think and Grow Rich*, says to "make your desires clear and reduce them to writing." By writing down a clear goal, you exponentially increase the likelihood of achieving that goal. I can't overemphasize the importance of knowing your personal **TM gap** or what impact that knowledge will have on all of your decisions. If you have the goal of becoming a **ME** or even a **TM**, knowing your individual estimated amounts will help you during times of frustration or doubt.

On a personal note . . .

The plan for my retirement was to leverage this lever to the fullest. I'm currently on track to accrue almost two years of sick leave and be eligible to retire when I am 54 years old. In my case, this lever alone will allow my wife and I to retire a **ME**. I'm not sure if I will retire at 54 or not, but I'll have that option. I will work with the retirement office to see what the exact payouts will be with different scenarios, then compare what other opportunities I may have after I retire and make the determination as to what option is best for our situation.

My wife, on the other hand, took fifteen years off from teaching. Because of this choice, her retirement will be much smaller, and she'll need to work until she's sixty years old to even start collecting. If everything goes as planned over the next decade, I will retire a **ME** and we will be in good shape to become a **TM** with just my retirement and the remaining levers that are discussed in the book. That doesn't count my wife's retirement, so anything she makes will only make it easier. If she and I continue to work hard, are disciplined, and persist with these levers, we're on track to become **TMs** despite raising a family of five kids with one teacher's income through fifteen years. This lever is powerful if we use it correctly!

Chapter 2

Lever 2—Make the Profession Pay You

The next lever that's available in greater degree to teachers than to people in other professions is the benefit of knowing exactly how much you'll make throughout your career. To some, this may be viewed as a constraint or a negative; after all, there isn't a chance to get a big, end-of-year bonus or have an incredible quarter that could greatly increase your earnings for the year. And let's be honest, knowing exactly how much you'll make this year and the next year and the year after that can be a little, well, boring. However, for the astute educator, this can be a huge advantage and a major lever that we can use to become a **ME** and eventually a **TM**. The perceptive educator will see this as an opportunity to make the profession pay more!

Before we get too far into discussing this lever, I'd like to remind you of the prerequisites that were discussed in the introduction of this book: **hard work**, **discipline**, and **persistence**. This lever will require all three of these prerequisites.

Now, let's take a look at this salary schedule from Georgia. The column to the left signifies how many years of experience the teacher has, and each subsequent column represents the degrees earned by the teacher (bachelor's, master's, specialist, and doctorate).[8] Does anything stand out to you?

Year's Experience	Bachelor's	Master's	Specialist	Doctorate
0	46,646	51,776	56,282	61,980
2	48,362	53,824	58,704	64,660
4	50,078	55,872	61,126	67,340
6	51,794	57,920	63,548	70,020
8	53,510	59,968	65,970	72,700
10	55,226	62,016	68,392	75,380
12	56,942	64,064	70,814	78,060
14	58,658	66,112	73,236	80,740
16	60,374	68,160	75,658	83,420
18	62,090	70,208	78,080	86,100
20	63,806	72,256	80,502	88,780
22	65,522	74,304	82,924	91,460
24	67,238	76,352	85,346	94,140
26	68,954	78,400	87,768	96,820
28+	70,670	80,448	90,190	99,500

When I look at this salary schedule, the first thing I think is that after twenty-eight years in the profession, I'd rather be in the doctorate column than in the bachelor's. That's almost $30,000 more for the same year of work! Another thing that stands out to me is that the first year in the profession for someone who has a doctorate makes more money than someone who has a bachelor's makes after fifteen years in the profession. It makes sense that the education profession would reward more education with a bigger salary. After all, we are in education. When looking at the salary schedule, you can clearly see the amount of money you would make (in 2020 dollars) at different points in your career. For every degree you earn, you get more money.

One definite way you can become a **ME** or a **TM** is to make more money during your career. If these are the rules of the game, why not make the profession pay you more by getting as many degrees as you can?

Keep getting those degrees!

When I was finishing my master's degree, I ran into a very successful uncle of mine at my brother's wedding. He was very interested in hearing about how I was finishing my master's degree. I still remember the advice he shouted out to me as he was driving away: "Keep getting those degrees!" I thought it was cool that he was excited for me, and his advice stayed with me. As my career has progressed, I'm very glad I followed his advice.

Now, before you run off and get every degree available, there are several factors you should consider. These might include the cost of the degree, how much time it takes to complete the degree, what the ROI (Return on Investment) is, and how much time you have before you retire. I've seen many teachers going about getting an extra degree the right way and others going about it the wrong way. You need to choose the right degree from the right university at the right time in your career. I would not advise you to chase the wrong degree for the wrong price at the wrong time, which can be avoided by carefully considering all the factors.

Factors to consider in the first ten years of your career

When you begin thinking about earning another degree, you should consider how much time you have left in the profession. If it's your first year teaching, you may want to wait a year before starting your next degree. Give yourself a year to get a feel of teaching, make a ton of mistakes, and learn all the lessons that your first year teaches you!

But after that first year or anytime during the first ten years in the profession, get back in school! The quicker you get your master's degree, the quicker you get that master's paycheck.

And then when you finish your master's degree, get back in school! Again, the quicker you get the next degree, the quicker you get the next degree's paycheck. You do not want to delay getting these advanced degrees if you're trying to become a **ME** or **TM**! In the words of Uncle Hugh, Keep getting those degrees!

Keep in mind that it takes about one and a half to three years to complete your master's degree and the same amount to complete your specialist degree (master's + thirty credit hours in some states). Depending on the school and how quickly you finish a dissertation, it can take another three or more years to complete a doctorate. That's an extra six to ten years of schooling. Some teachers choose to go from the master's degree directly to their doctorate degree and skip the specialist degree all together. This is the most efficient path to take with time and money because you can skip the cost associated with the specialist degree and finish your education quicker, getting you to that last column on the pay scale quicker.

These degrees can be expensive and time consuming, but if you get them within your first ten years, the ROI makes them well worth it. If you have twenty years left in your career, you'll earn between $104,000 and $176,000 more *per degree* over the course of those twenty years. If you go from a bachelors to a doctorate degree in the first ten years of your career, you'll earn almost $450,000 more in the final twenty years of your career than if you didn't continue your education. And as we've already seen, earning more also affects your retirement payouts. This is powerful stuff!

Factors to consider in the second ten years of your career

If you're in the second ten years of your career, you may want to pay a little more attention to the number of degrees you should earn and see if the ROI is sufficient to justify the costs. Like I mentioned earlier, these degrees are an investment of time and money, and you want to make sure they'll earn back the money you invested and then some. A master's degree will cost anywhere from $10,000 to $30,000 depending on what program you choose. A specialist will cost you a little more, and a doctorate will cost even more. I don't share those numbers to discourage you in any way, but you do need to make sure earning more degrees makes sense financially the further you get into your career.

I pointed out that with twenty years left in your career, you would earn an additional $104,000 to $176,000 over the remainder of your career. If you finished your degrees later and only had ten years left in your career, you would earn between $97,000 and $101,000 more than if you only had a bachelor's degree. When you consider the cost of the degree with the diminished amount you would earn, it may not make sense to get to the doctorate column, but it may still make sense to earn a master's or specialist degree depending on the cost and your situation.

Factors to consider in the last ten years of your career

If you're at this point in your career, you really want to examine how much time you plan on working and how much the degree will cost. Look at your district's salary schedule closely and do the math. It may only be worth getting a master's if you currently have a bachelors or a specialist if you currently have a master's degree and you only have five to eight years left in your career. Don't forget to factor in how much more you'll get in your retirement while making this decision (60% of a larger salary for the rest of your life). It's okay if it doesn't make financial sense to get the next degree; you simply would need to focus on the remaining levers to make sure that you make **ME** or **TM** status.

A Real-Life Example from a Teacher

I recently had a conversation with a teacher who was finishing her specialist degree. This degree corresponds to column three in the salary schedule. She was a younger teacher in her sixth year of teaching, and I asked her if she was going to continue going to school and earn her doctorate when she finished her specialist degree. She gave a sigh and said she was tired of going to school and working full time as an elementary teacher. She told me that it really wasn't worth it for earning $5,000 more.

I asked her where she got that number, and she told me that she'd glanced at the salary schedule. I pulled up the salary schedule and a calculator, and we began to talk. I pointed out that if she took four more years to finish her doctorate degree, she would be making $7,000 more ($2,000 more than she thought). Then, I pointed out to her that the difference between the specialist and the doctorate degrees grows each year, and in the twenty-eighth year, it would be a difference of $9,000. If we took the average of $8,000 a year and multiplied it by the twenty years left she had until she retired, she would earn $160,000 more than if she didn't earn a doctorate. The look on her face began to change, and I could see that she was rethinking the possibility getting the next degree.

I then asked this teacher how long she planned on living. She looked confused, then laughed and said that she didn't know. For the easier math, we agreed that she would live to the age of ninety. I showed her the difference of what the payout from her retirement plan with a doctorate degree would be as opposed to if she stopped her studies with a specialist degree. The difference turned out to be $195,510 more. I asked her if a few more years of effort was worth $355,510 dollars over the rest of her life. She was shocked to see a number so much bigger than the $5,000 she thought she would get.

Definition of luck

I love the roman philosopher Seneca's definition of luck. He said, "Luck is what happens when preparation meets opportunity." I love this definition because it rightly assigns the individual some influence on what happens in their life rather than luck being some mystical force that picks winners and losers. If you think about it, opportunities are flying around us at all times. I have a friend who seems to get the best deals on everything! I always get jealous and tell him he's a lucky dog. The truth of the matter is that he researches whatever he's going to buy. He learns everything about it and where the best deals are. He even goes an extra step and takes really good care of his purchases and then sells the items on eBay when he is finished with them. He often makes a profit on the item after using it for a time. It's easy to assign his good fortune on random luck, but it's more accurate to say he puts forth a great deal of preparation and recognizes opportunities that are there for everyone if they prepare their eyes to see it.

PREPARATION + OPPORTUNITY = LUCK

I share Seneca's definition of luck because earning more degrees, working hard, being disciplined, and being persistent are going to help you recognize and be prepared for many opportunities during your career. Some might call these opportunities lucky breaks, or they might explain it away as district politics. In reality, these positions are the convergence of preparation and opportunity. These opportunities can help you make this profession pay you more and help you become a **ME** or **TM** if you are lucky—I mean, prepared.

Be strategic in your career path

I've shared a lot of salaries in this chapter to illustrate having higher education will make this profession pay you more. All the salaries to this point have been based on a teacher's salary schedule.

As you acquire all the knowledge and expertise that comes with earning additional degrees, you will find that many opportunities in education will become available to you. You may even find yourself asking the question, "To leave the classroom, or not to leave the classroom?"

For some, leaving the classroom means going into an instructional coach position or a district position. For others, leaving the classroom means going into administration. In many cases, leaving the classroom means your contract will require you to work more days in the year.

This can also put you on a different salary schedule altogether, which typically equates to earning more money. In my district, these positions mean you can move from a 190-day employee schedule to a 210-day employee schedule, and eventually it could lead to a twelve-month schedule. Many of the non-administrative instructional coaching positions maintain the same per diem pay rate, but the extra days on the contract translate to much more income during each year worked and throughout retirement.

Example #1

Janita was an amazing math teacher in the classroom for twenty years. She earned a specialist degree and enjoyed leading the professional development opportunities for her school. The district math coach position eventually became available, and she decided to interview for it. She was thrilled and a little scared when she learned she got the job. She also learned that the position paid the same per diem, but it was a 210-day contract—twenty days more than when she was in the classroom—which meant she made the profession pay her more overall!

Janita's scenario:

20 day more contract x $423 per Diem = $8,460 more

$8,460 x 10 more years to retirement = $84,600 more

$8,460 x 60% in retirement = $5,076 more every year
of retirement

$5,076 X 30 years of retirement = $152,280

$84,600 in career + $152,280 in retirement =
$236,880 more!

Janita got the most out of this lever by making a slight shift in her career. She recognized math was her niche, and she was ready when the opportunity presented itself. Some might call that luck, but we'll call it preparation.

Example #2

Shelton was a talented ESOL (English to Speakers of Other Languages) teacher with five years left in his career. He had toyed with the idea of administration for years, but he enjoyed the classroom and was waiting for the right time and the right situation to take that step.

Eventually, he heard of an intriguing opportunity and interviewed for an assistant principal position in a school with a high ESOL population. This position came with a $10,000 raise. He got the job and loved working at the new school in this exciting new facet of the education profession. He jumped in with both feet, learned a ton, and continued to grow in experience and confidence.

Lever 2—Make the profession pay you

Two years later, he heard of another opportunity in the neighboring district. This district paid $20,000 more for the same position, and the contract was twenty more days a year. Shelton worked for three years in the neighboring district and retired at fifty-five years old.

In five years, he went from making $70,000 a year to his final contract of $100,000 a year. Shelton made $80,000 more in his last five years of work than he would have had he stayed in the classroom, and now he'll make more throughout retirement too.

Shelton's scenario:

$30,000 more X 60% retirement = $18,000 more every year in retirement

$18,000 X 30 years of retirement = $540.000

$540,000 in retirement + $80,000 in career = $620,000 more!

Shelton made a shift in the twilight of his career, leveraged his knowledge and experience with ESOL students, and increased his income more than a half a million dollars over the rest of his life! Some might say he was lucky, but I would say his preparation met a couple opportunities.

Teachers sometimes struggle with the prospect of leaving the classroom and that's fine. I'm simply suggesting that you leave the door open for possible opportunities that are there for the taking if you're prepared. Whatever your interest is, the key for you is to leverage your passions and talents and find your niche. What do you do better than most in the teaching profession? Identify those talents and passions and then look for ways to make that talent pay you.

The law of attraction

Much has been written about the law of attraction, which basically states that whatever we focus on, we will attract into our lives. Rhonda Byrne explains this law of attraction in her bestselling book *The Secret*. Napoleon Hill also taps into this concept in his classic book on finance *Think and Grow Rich*. Hill claims that you

What you focus on, you will attract into your life

must think about and focus on the goals you have and then so that the likelihood of achieving them will be increased.[9] As you go throughout your career focused on growing as a teacher and developing your talents, more opportunities will come your way. The opportunities will be attracted to you like iron to a magnet. If you neglect your talents and misplace your focus from growing and developing, or, even worse, if you reject opportunities when they present themselves, opportunities will not be attracted to you.

This attraction is true with money as well as with opportunities. The teaching profession offers so many opportunities to develop your skills, and those opportunities often end with you earning more money. There are opportunities to teach Saturday school, extra periods, and summer school; There are opportunities to tutor, sell tickets at school events, and review curriculum; there are even opportunities to participate in pilot or adoption teams, proctoring tests, create assessments, teach at the local college, stay after school for detention, etc. I'm amazed at how many opportunities, and the associated money, teachers reject. If you reject opportunities and money, you're not using the law of attraction for your benefit. Some might even say that if you reject opportunities and money, opportunities and money will reject you. But if you focus on opportunities for growth and extra money, opportunities and money have a weird way of being very attracted to you. You might even say that your preparation and the opportunities will make you lucky.

If you consistently combine getting extra degrees, taking opportunities for extra cash, and making strategic career moves for higher earning jobs, then the amount of extra income you'll earn over your career and throughout your retirement is astounding! That extra money makes this a very powerful lever to use on your way to becoming a **ME**, and it might even be enough to help you become a **TM** yourself. All this is possible through hard work, discipline, and persistence.

Multiple Streams of Income

I'd like to point out that the teaching contract is generally a 190-day contract for the entire year. This means that you have an additional 175 days in the year that are available for using your skills and talents to generate streams of income from sources other than teaching. You can also look for other streams of income in side jobs throughout the year. I know teachers who coach in summer camps and summer leagues, teachers who drive buses at Boy Scout camps, and teachers who start businesses employing the very skills that they use in teaching. The point is that there is a lot of time available during which a teacher can explore additional streams of income to increase the probability of becoming a **ME** and even a **TM**.

One exciting aspect of the numbers I've shared is that they are based on the assumption that there's only one teaching income in the household! This is a lot of money for one household—well above the national average. If there *is* another stream of income by way of a significant other or additional streams of income, these dollar amounts will be higher!

On a personal note . . .

Over the years, this has been a lever that I've tried to use to my advantage. I looked at that pay scale when I first started teaching, and it did not take long to figure out that I needed to get as far over to the right column as quickly as possible. Even though it took longer for me to finish my bachelor's degree, I quickly finished my master's degree, worked on an add-on degree in administration and finished my doctorate degree before I turned thirty-three. After finishing my doctorate, I began teaching as an adjunct professor of education for a local college. I've either been going to school or working two jobs (my day job and teaching evening college classes) my entire career.

I really believe that if you reject money, money will reject you. This means I can hardly turn down an opportunity to make more money. When I was an assistant principal, I took every Saturday school and after-school help session opportunity that came up. I volunteered for the summer school director position every year. One year, I made $12,000 extra because of all the opportunities my school offered that none of the other assistant principals wanted.

In fact, one summer I was at the neighborhood pool, and I over-heard one of our good neighbors complaining that she couldn't find anyone to mow her lawn. I half-jokingly told her that I would do it for $10 a mow. She knew she couldn't beat that price, and she yelled "Deal!" before I could take it back.

Lever 2—Make the profession pay you

Now I was in a predicament. I say that I believe that if you reject money, then money will reject you. Here, money was staring me in the face. Was I going to reject it? Well, I mowed her lawn for two summers, and she loved to tell everyone that her lawn boy had a doctorate. I still can't pass up an opportunity if it comes my way.

My wife is the same way. Even though she left the profession for fifteen years, she took the opportunities that came knocking when she could. She tutored students after school, and she helped other families when they needed someone to watch their children. She and I completed our master's degrees before our kids started coming every three years. Now that our kids are older and in school, my wife has returned to the classroom as a Spanish teacher. Just this past break, she accepted an opportunity to work on some modules for the Social Studies department for an extra $1,000. If you're wondering why a Spanish teacher was working on the school's Social Studies modules, it was because none of the Social Studies teachers wanted the opportunity.

Even though we've generally made the profession pay us and we've used the law of attraction in our benefit, I wanted to share our thought process regarding my wife's next degree. We've done the math and looked at what the impact would be on the family if she were to get her next degree. She's determined that there are too many unknowns in our life for her to pursue that degree at this time. In the future, the situation may change, which would change the calculus on that decision, but for now, she's not ready to take on that adventure. I share that to illustrate how these decisions are individual to each family.

But if you work hard, are disciplined, and persist, you can make this profession pay you.

The Millionaire and Me

Chapter 3

Lever 3—Tell Your Money What to Do

N othing could be more exciting than the topic of this important chapter. Ok, maybe I'm overhyping this a bit. I mean, who gets excited about living on a budget? Yes, I said the b-word. That's what I mean when I say, "Tell your money what to do!" It just sounds a lot tougher to say that than "budget." All jokes aside, we really need to be good at using this lever. There's no viable substitute.

I know people often view living on a budget like going on a diet. They may see it as constrictive, painful, and not a lot of fun. Or even worse, they might be apathetic and simply don't want to do it. I want to remind you that we cannot approach this lever with that mindset. We're trying to achieve excellence here!

In his book *Take the Stairs: 7 Steps to Achieving True Success*, Rory Vaden reminds us that "successful people have the self-discipline to do things they don't want to do. They do the things they don't want to do *even when* they don't *feel like* doing them."[10]

We'll have to use this lever even when we don't feel like using it. In fact, without this lever, it is almost impossible to become a **ME**

(Millionaire Equivalent) or a **TM** (True Millionaire). This lever, like the others, relies on the three prerequisites of hard work, discipline, and persistence.

Advice from Two Uncles

Even though we didn't have a lot of money in my house as a kid, I was blessed with an amazing family and extended family. I've already shared with you the one piece of advice that my Uncle Hugh gave me when he learned I was finishing my master's degree: "Keep getting those degrees!" That wasn't the only bit of advice he offered me. He gave me and my wife another wonderful pearl of wisdom when we got married, saying that the difference in marital happiness between spending $50 more than you make each month and spending $50 less than you make each month is immeasurable. The advice is profound in its simplicity.

The $ you make < The $ you spend = Bad, Unhappy

The $ you make > The $ you spend = Good, Happy

I think it's noteworthy that my uncle didn't mention how much money I needed to make. It didn't matter if we made $30,000 a year or $300,000 a year; he said that if we spent $50 more than we made, we'd be heading for trouble. It's only $50, but if you consistently spend more than you make, your spending habits will lead to a great deal of unhappiness. Conversely, if you consistently spend less than you make, your spending habits will relieve you of so much stress and heartache, and they will bring a peace to you and your family, not to mention spending less than you make is the only way to become a **ME** and eventually close the **TM gap**.

Uncle Hugh wasn't the only uncle dishing out the knowledge; I received another piece of advice from my Uncle Lamar. He spent a career working in education, and when he learned I was going to be a teacher, he pulled me aside and asked, "You want to be a teacher? The only way you will make any money in teaching is if you *save*!" This was another statement that was profound because of its simplicity.

This advice is directly tied to the benefit we have in our profession of knowing exactly how much we'll make throughout our career. Since we know how much we can make, creating a budget is less complicated, which makes it easier to plan for saving.

Teaching as a profession + Saving $ = Retiring rich!

The Snake River Plains

Whenever I think of a budget, my mind goes back to when I was a teenager. Every summer, my younger brother and I would move to Idaho and work on my grandfather's farm in a very dry and sandy region of southeastern Idaho. My brother and I lived on the farm with our grandfather and worked on everything that needed to be done. The days were long and hot. It was an amazing time that I look back on with great fondness now, but it was tough work.

One chore we had to do every morning and evening was move irrigation pipe in multiple fields—usually fields of hay, wheat, or famous Idaho potatoes. The process of moving the pipe consisted of moving a quarter mile to a half mile line of an irrigation or sprinkler pipe to an adjacent section of the field. These long lines of sprinkler pipe consisted of thirty to forty individual pipes that were connected at the ends. Each individual pipe was twenty-five feet long and two to four inches in diameter. Then, each pipe had a three- to four-foot riser pipe attached midway across with an industrial sprinkler-head connected at the top that sprayed water in a twenty-five- to forty-foot-wide circle.

In order to move a line of pipe, we would disconnect the first twenty-five-foot pipe from the main line at the head of the field. Then, we would pick the pipe up and move it over to the next section, usually forty feet down the field. We would reconnect one end of that section to the main line and then return for the next twenty-five-foot pipe, continuing the process until we finished moving the entire line. We would spend hours moving these pipelines to ensure that the field received the life-giving water the crops required.

Even though the region is very dry and windy, the Snake River Plains are dotted with green fields of hay, barley, wheat, and potatoes. This is only possible because of the elaborate canal system that moves the water from the Snake River throughout the entire region and because of the farmers who make sure the water only goes where it's needed.

The entire livelihood of the region depends on the farmers and engineers being very intentional in making the water go where they need it to go. In fact, McDonalds would not be able to provide their delicious french fries to the entire world if the people of the Snake River Plains in Southeastern Idaho did not take the water from the Snake River, make it travel through a complex system of canals and pipes of various sizes, then spread it onto the crops miles away from the river. If the farmers didn't purposely assign a portion of the water for specific purposes, the water would go about its merry way to the Pacific Ocean, and the region would only be covered with unproductive sagebrush rather than prosperous fields.

What does this story have to do with a budget you ask? Much like the farmers and engineers in the Snake River Plains assign specific amounts of water to specific purposes and places, we must assign specific amounts of our monthly paycheck to specific purposes and places—otherwise known as budgeting. If we fail to do this, our money will go about its merry way, and it's almost guaranteed that the money won't be productive. Without a plan, like the old proverb says, "A fool and his money are soon parted." As Benjamin Franklin once said, "If you fail to plan, you are planning to fail."

Failing to plan = Planning to fail

Many financial gurus throughout the years have addressed the importance of creating a plan that helps you not be like the fool who is soon parted from his or her money.

George Clason, in his classic book on finance *The Richest Man in Babylon*, shares the concept of making your money work for you. He says you should give your money specific jobs to do, and if your money's not profitable in performing its duties, it should be dispatched somewhere else.[11]

Dave Ramsey says that we should "give each dollar a name," explaining that we should assign specific assignments to every dollar before the check even comes in. Some dollars are given the assignment to take care of utilities, others are given the assignment of putting gas in your car, and still other dollars are given the assignment of feeding your family. Every dollar is given an assignment and is accounted for.[12]

Earlier, I referenced the concept of Prodigious Accumulators of Wealth (PAWs) that Dr. Stanley and Dr. Danko explained in their seminal work *The Millionaire Next Door*. The first-generation millionaires in this study were able to accumulate great wealth as a result of their ability to live within their means, make a plan, and stick to their plan. The researchers were surprised to learn that around 80% of the millionaires they studied were first-generation millionaires and that many of these millionaires were meticulous budgeters.[13]

David Bach, in his book *The Automatic Millionaire: A Powerful One-Step Plan to Live and Finish Rich*, suggests putting everything on autopay. This includes your contributions to your emergency fund and to charitable giving.[14]

Bach also suggests that you pay yourself 10% every month to invest, making sacrifices like cutting out frivolous expenses to make this automatic 10% possible. You can decide for yourself what you determine to be frivolous, whether it be a morning latte, cable, or reoccurring subscriptions. The point Bach tries to make is that you need to find 10% of your budget to save and invest. By making these contributions and payments automatic, you remove the guesswork, and you'll more easily become an automatic millionaire.

Mark Victor Hansen and Robert Allen, in their book *The One Minute Millionaire: The Enlightened Way to Wealth*, say that wealthy people possess seven skills that Hansen and Allen refer to as MoneySkills. These MoneySkills are as follows:

MoneySkill #1 – Value: Each dollar bill as a money seed.

MoneySkill #2 – Control: control your money to the penny.

MoneySkill #3 – Save: Save at least 10% of the money you earn.

MoneySkill #4 – Invest: Have a system for investing your money.

MoneySkill #5 – Earn: Have Multiple Streams of Income outside of your job.

MoneySkill #6 – Shield: Protect yourself with legal entities.

MoneySkill #7 – Share: Donate at least 10% of your income.[15]

Many other authors and researchers have likewise highlighted the absolute necessity of budgeting in order to accumulate wealth. There are numerous strategies on how to budget. Some suggest the envelope system, where you cut all of your credit cards and pay for everything with cash that has been separated into different envelopes for every category in your budget. Other people suggest apps or spreadsheets to help organize your budget to ensure that your "water" gets to your "crops," meaning your money does what you tell it to do.

There are also different philosophies on how much you budget for each purpose and when to spend in each category. Elizabeth Warren suggested in her book *All Your Worth: The Ultimate Lifetime Money Plan* that you should use 50% of your after-tax salary for your needs, 30% for your wants, and 20% for your investments, or pay-yourself-first money.[16] If your needs consititute more than 50% of your take-home pay, you may need to downsize, reevaluate the definition of "must have," or adjust the next category. For your wants, Warren doesn't want you to live too frugally, but she still says you need to keep those things within a budget. Then, if you pay yourself 20% of your income every month, you're going to be in great shape for retiring as a **ME** or a **TM**!

Another philosophy that's sometimes mentioned in literature is to pay God first 5% to 10%(charitable giving), pay yourself 10% to 20% second (retirement savings), and then allocate the remaining 70% to 85% to your needs and wants (Housing, debt, food, entertainment etc.). This is similar to the Warren's suggestion, except it includes the concept of budgeting your charitable giving as a priority. It's up to you to research and workshop the secret combination of strategies and percentages for your specific situation and values. The only thing that's essential is that you *use a budget* and that you *stick to your budget*.

The following are common components of a solid budget that appear in most financial literature:

Pay yourself first

Most financial gurus and books identify the concept of paying yourself first as key to accumulating wealth. But what does it mean to pay yourself first? Isn't someone else paying me? The answer is simple: You pay yourself by putting money aside to save and by investing for retirement every time you earn money. From every paycheck you earn, you *must* set aside money from that paycheck for yourself. These funds can then be invested in interest bearing accounts to be used in the future. Most financial experts recommend that a minimum of 10% of every paycheck be put in this category. They suggest that this percentage should be increased up to 15%-20% of every paycheck if you don't have debt.

These pay-yourself-first funds are crucial for what we'll discuss in the next chapter. You may recall the **TM gap** we discussed in chapter two. This is the gap between what your pension will produce each year and what a **TM**'s IRA would produce each year. In the scenarios from chapter two, we saw that the **TM gap** of our examples ranged from $10,000 to $40,000 each year. This means that the people in the examples needed to have enough money saved outside their pensions to produce $10,000 to $40,000 every year. You cannot become a **ME** and close the **TM gap** without consistently paying yourself first! We'll go deeper into this in the next chapter.

> **You cannot become a ME and close the TM gap without paying yourself first!**

Build an emergency fund

This is different from paying yourself. An emergency fund is for the hiccups that happen in life. I don't know about you, but every time I get a raise or an extra opportunity for money, it seems like something around the house breaks, there's car trouble, or something else goes wrong. This emergency fund exists for those boo-boos or uh-ohs. Some people suggest you have anywhere from $1,000 to six months' salary for this fund. Whatever the amount you decide on, if you have a healthy emergency fund, you're more likely to succeed at the next topic.

Identify your needs and wants

A key component of a budget is correctly identifying your needs and wants. Needs are things you must have, and wants are things that are nice but not absolutely necessary. If you boil it down to the most basic components, your needs would likely fall into the following categories: food, shelter, clothing, transportation, and insurance. Wants could fall somewhere within each one of those categories and then everything outside of those categories. In developing your budget, you decide what you can afford within the needs category and then which things you can afford within your wants category. For example, you need a house for a family of three, but you may want a house with ten bedrooms and a heated pool—something you can't afford. Or you need to eat, but you may want to eat in a restaurant every day. People get into trouble when, for whatever reason, they confuse their wants for their needs and don't live within the plan they created by way of a budget. In short, they end up spending more than they make.

It may be hard to believe that it can be that simple, but by correctly identifying needs and wants and budgeting for each appropriately, you will be able to pay yourself first the minimum recommended 10% or more. If you do this, you will easily become a **ME** and even a **TM**.

When we mess up and don't make a budget, don't follow a budget, or don't make our emergency fund big enough, debt happens.

Pay off outstanding debt as soon as possible

If you happen to be a typical human being in the 21st century, you probably already have debt. If you have debt, you have to get out of that hole. Debt eats the money that should be working for you! This applies to any debt you may be carrying. I use the word *carrying* on purpose; you're literally carrying a load with debt that inhibits you from achieving your goal of becoming a **T**rue **M**illionaire. Debt slows your progress! It doesn't matter if the debt is in the form of credit cards, student loans, home loans, Home Equity Line of Credit (HELOC), car loans, financed furniture or appliances, or loans from your rich sister; when you're in debt, you're paying today and tomorrow for goods and services that have been rendered in the past rather than saving up for the future.

One way many financial experts suggest for getting rid of current debt is to line up all your debts from the highest interest rate to the lowest interest rate and then pay them off in that order. They also recommend consolidating all your high interest debt into no interest or lower interest options. Sometimes, you can consolidate a high interest credit card into another credit card that will give you a year of 0% interest on transfers. When you do the math, this is the most cost-effective way to pay off more debts with the same dollars you would have spent on the debt.

Another way some financial experts suggest for paying off debt is to line up all of your debt from the smallest amount to the largest amount and pay off your debt in that order regardless of the percentage rates. They claim there is power in accomplishing a small goal quickly and that power will create momentum for tackling the next highest amount. They say that even if you could potentially pay more in interest, you'll make up the difference by getting the quick victories and being motivated to finish the drill. Confidence comes from repeated success, and these small, repeated victories give you the confidence to keep going. Dave Ramsey refers to this as a debt snowball and says that when the snowball gets momentum, there's no stopping it.[17]

It doesn't matter which strategy you study out and decide on implementing. What matters is that you study the strategy, choose the one you believe in, and implement it consistently. The quicker you pay off your debt, the quicker you'll become a **ME** and eventually a **TM**!

Do not go into debt!

Now that we understand the core components of a budget, you can put one into place that meets you needs. Make sure you have the correct percentages for paying yourself first, building a sufficient emergency fund, covering your needs and wants, and paying off any outstanding debt. With all of these components in place, I want to return to the importance of not accumulating more debt.

I almost titled this section "Avoid debt," but I decided that wasn't strong enough, so I changed it to the command form: "Do not go into debt!" It makes sense that in order to become a **ME** and a **TM** you'll need to accumulate wealth. Just like it's really hard to fill a bucket with water if you have a hole in the bottom of the bucket, it's really hard to accumulate wealth if your money is leaving your account to pay off debt. Accumulating debt is the opposite of accumulating wealth.

I'm sorry to tell you that this aspect of the lever will require you to tell yourself the most awful word in the English language: *no*. You shouldn't buy something unless you've budgeted for it. I know this approach may not be popular, and there are some who say there is good debt in addition to bad debt. Some financial gurus talk about leveraging debt to produce income, and others are adamant about never using debt. I'm not getting into that debate, but I will encourage you to treat debt like an annoying neighbor and avoid it.

Most financial advisors agree that you shouldn't carry a balance on your credit cards. Most balances on credit cards are from consumables (food, clothes, furniture, vacations, gifts, etc.) that were purchased and not budgeted for. It's not wise to rob from your future to pay for things that you didn't budget for now.

I had a good friend once tell me his trick to determine if he could afford a purchase. He said, "If I have the money in my pocket, I can afford it. If I don't have the money in my pocket, I can't." It may be simplistic to look at it this way, but why should we make this complicated? When it comes to buying things that you need or want, save for it, and pay cash. Don't go into debt for it.

My father used to tell me all the time that "there are two types of people: those who understand interest and those who don't. Those who don't understand it, pay it. Those who do understand it, earn it!" Debt would make you the type of person who

> **There are two types of people: those who understand interest and those who don't. Those who don't understand interest, pay it!**
>
> **- My dad**

doesn't understand interest; you'd be the type of person who pays it. The debt industry isn't a multitrillion-dollar industry by accident. It's a multitrillion-dollar industry because there are a ton of people who don't understand interest, and they pay a ton of it to various companies. When you go into debt, you're spending more for the item than the asking price because you pay interest in addition to the cost of the item.

Have you ever gone to a store to buy something, and when you go to the register to pay for the item, you tell the cashier you insist on paying more than the asking price? I know I haven't! But that's exactly what we do if we buy things on credit.

Credit Cards

Let's illustrate how we pay much more for items than their asking price with a credit card example:

Sam didn't have a plan or cash in his pocket. Instead of following a budget, he purchased many items using his credit card without much thought. He used his credit card on things like clothes, an evening out with friends, or other perceived needs and wants. He didn't have the money in his pocket, but he bought things anyway, opting for immediate gratification instead of a creating a plan and sticking to it. Even though, alone, the purchases were not big or extravagant, together, they added up quickly. Before he realized it, Sam had fallen into a debt trap and accumulated $2,000 debt on his credit cards.

The minimum payment on Sam's credit card was 3% of the principal or $10, whichever was higher. Sam only paid the minimum each month. Each month, his credit card charged him 20%

annual interest on his outstanding balance. When Sam made his payments, part of those payments went to paying interest and part went to the principal amount.

This is what Sam's credit card debt looked like after one month:

- Sam started with a credit card balance of **$2,000**

- Sam made a minimum payment of **$60** (3% of remaining balance)

- The credit card company applied part of the payment to interest: ($2,000 x 20% ÷ 12 months = **$33.33**)

- The credit card company applied part of the payment to principal ($60 - $33.33 = **$26.67**)

- This left a remaining balance of **$1,973.33** ($2,000 - $26.67)[18]

You can see that the remaining balance didn't go down much. If Sam paid only the minimum payment on the original $2,000 every month, it would take him over fifteen years to pay off the balance. When all was said and done, Sam would have paid **$4,241**, which is **$2,241** more than the original $2,000.00 credit card bill.

In the previous chapter, we mentioned the law of attraction, which claims that what you think about is attracted to you. We discussed how a corollary concept of that law might be that what you reject would then reject you. Another way to think about this concept would be that if you disrespect something, that thing might disrespect you, including money. Going into consumer debt disrespects money and will cause money to disrespect you.

A common debt trap people fall into is making money decisions based on whether they can afford the payments. Might I remind you of what my friend said? "If [you] have the money in your pocket, then [you] can afford it. If [you] do not have the money in your pocket, [you] can't afford it." Notice he didn't say, "If you can afford the *payments*."

Payments are the Siren's Song luring you into the rocks!

Payments are deceptive. They're the siren's song luring you into the rocks! Ok, maybe that's a little dramatic, but they do tend to ensnare the very people who think they'll benefit from payments. For example, the other day I visited my local Walmart and checked out the TV section. The TVs were so big and beautiful, and I just pictured them hanging on my wall with a beautiful sound system belting out an action movie or a football game. As I looked this time, I couldn't believe how much the prices have dropped over the years. You can get a huge, beautiful TV for $900! Just a few years ago, they cost thousands of dollars.

As I was marveling at how much you can buy now for relatively little compared to the past, my heart sank when I saw that on the tag right next to the price, our friends at Walmart had advertised a $29 monthly payment in the same size font as the price. I thought to myself, "Wow, I can have this beautiful TV in my house for $29 a month." Then I looked closer at the fine print and saw that the interest rate on those payments was 20%! That's ridiculous!

Do not be lured by payments of any kind for any purchase. People put furniture, phones, and appliances on payments, and there at Walmart I saw you could even put an affordable TV on a payment.

These payments add up and cause you to pay so much more for the item over time that it boggles the mind. Getting into debt thinking it makes the item more affordable will destroy your ability to accumulate wealth. If you don't have the money in your pocket, or in other words if you haven't budgeted for it and saved for it, then you can't afford it.

Cars

Now, let's talk about cars. The same principle should apply to cars. In most cases, cars are probably the second biggest purchase we'll make, second only to a house. The only difference is that your house grows in value over time, and your car decreases in value the moment you drive it off the lot.

Many new teachers love to reward themselves with a new car when they graduate and get their first real job. They've worked hard through school, graduated, and landed their dream job in their dream school. They deserve to splurge a little bit, right?

Wrong!

I've seen this scenario play out over and over again. New cars are expensive. Insurance on new cars is more expensive than insurance on older, cheaper cars. In theory, new cars shouldn't break down as often, but even routine maintenance and repairs on new cars are more expensive. And a lot of new cars make you use premium gas for heaven's sake!

Just walk through the parking lot of any school across the nation, and you'll see some nice cars! Many of them are financed with horrible terms and are eating way too much of the teacher's salary.

Those cars are eating away the teacher's ability to pay themselves first and to accumulate wealth.

Instead of getting into debt and acquiring a monthly bill for a liability that depreciates every day, many financial advisors suggest paying cash for a reasonable automobile. You can then save the money you would've spent on monthly payments for a better car in the future that you can pay for with cash, again, when you have saved enough. You could use the money saved from not paying interest to pay off other debt or build your emergency fund. Even better, you can give yourself a raise and increase the percentage of your pay-yourself-first funds. Going into debt should be avoided at all costs!

Exemptions to the rule

Possible exemptions to this rule of not going into debt are houses and additional degrees that will definitely pay you back with an ROI. It would be awesome if you were able to purchase these big items with cash, and many people do, but if you're unable to, get as big of a down payment as possible, pay for the most reasonable option available, and focus on paying it off as soon as possible.

As far as getting additional degrees in education is concerned, I suggest that you find the best option available for your area. You may want to consider the price, the convenience, the opportunities to network with colleagues in your district, etc. Most people don't consider the opportunities to network when they look at getting another degree, but the relationships you form in these groups often translate into opportunities down the line.

In order to avoid debt, you'll need to consistently exercise that prerequisite of discipline and persistence. You may mess up and make an impulse buy. You may think you have to have that new sofa, the granite countertops, or the dream vacation. Or you may have an emergency that's bigger than your emergency fund! If any of that happens, just get back up, recommit, dig yourself out of the hole, and avoid stepping in another hole at all costs. If you need clarity or motivation to avoid debt, I suggest you read books or listen to podcasts from any of the authors I've mentioned, and that can help motivate you to stay strong.

Returning to Snake River Plains

Let's finish this chapter like we started and return to our analogy of the Snake River Plains. All the financial experts I've mentioned in this chapter are like the engineers who built the canal system to take the water from the Snake River to different areas. You're like the farmer who needs to extract the water from the canal and take it to your crops. You have to work hard, exercise discipline, and be persistent. If you consistently make the water go where you need it to go, your crops will grow! If you consistently pay yourself first, avoid debt, have a sufficient emergency fund, and budget for your needs and wants, you'll have much less stress and much more peace in your life, and you'll be in great shape to become a **ME** and ultimately a **TM**!

On a personal note . . .

I would love to tell you that my family and I have lived faithfully on a budget throughout my teaching career. I would love to tell you that we never splurged on a vacation or made an impulse buy. I would love to tell you that we never financed an automobile.

Of course, none of those statements would be true. We had cars break down at inopportune times; we had appliances break and didn't have enough in the emergency fund to pay for new ones; we had kids need braces, glasses, and hearing aids that we didn't budget for—I mean, who would have guessed the rascal was going to fail his hearing test in second grade? We thought he was just ignoring us.

In short, we had life happen.

I *can* tell you that when cars and appliances did break down, we got the most reasonable ones for the most reasonable price we could find. And because we consistently followed the principles outlined in this chapter, we always had very good credit, which allowed us to get the best financing available. And we always paid the cars and appliances off as soon as possible. In fact, it never took more than two years.

While accruing money for our future has been important to us, we also feel it's important to give, so we've consistently given to charities. We were more or less disciplined in paying ourselves first because we set our account up to pay the money automatically every month. Even though we did a great job of setting it up automatically, we were not always paying ourselves what we deserved. We were not saving 10% to 20% of our income at first, but we increased the amount when we realized we were missing the mark.

Lever 3—Tell Your Money What to Do

Over the years, I would say that this lever has been the one that we have struggled with the most. Most of the time, we were successful in forcing the money to do what we wanted and needed it to do. Sometimes, the money went where *it* wanted to go instead, or there simply wasn't enough for our needs. But we consistently adjusted our needs to the money available and kept moving forward. With hard work, discipline, and persistence, our fields are greener than they were yesterday, and we're preparing for a great harvest come fall.

The Millionaire and Me

Chapter 4

Lever 4—Put Your Money To Work

Now that you've done the hard work, shown great discipline, and been persistent in telling your money what to do by means of a budget, you should have money set aside each month to invest. Now it's time to put that money to work for you, which will make it possible for you to close the **TM gap** and become a **T**rue **M**illionaire yourself. The power of this lever comes directly from putting to work all the money that comes from paying yourself first every month over the span of your working career! If you were not disciplined and persistent in paying yourself throughout your career, the power of this lever is greatly diminished. But if you were disciplined and persistent, you can close the **TM gap**!

You may recall Doug, Katrina, and Suzanne from the examples in chapter one. They each worked a varying number of years, which resulted in different fixed amounts in the payouts they will receive during retirement. Yet each one of our examples had a gap between what their retirements would provide and what the amount a **TM**'s IRA produces each year. Remember that our **TM** has $1,000,000 in a retirement account that earns 8% interest a year, which comes to $80,000 each year. With this lever, we'll take the money accrued through good budgeting (Lever 3) and close the gap between what we would earn in retirement and what the **TM**'s yearly payout is. It is with this lever that we become a Millionaire Equivalent (**ME**).

You may remember that Doug got into teaching at age twenty-nine and didn't get any additional degrees. He had a successful career and retired before he turned sixty! In order to become a **ME**, Doug would need to produce $80,000 a year from his retirement and other sources. His retirement would produce $42,600 a year, leaving him with a **TM gap** of $37,400. He had the largest **TM gap** of all of our examples that he needed to fill.

Doug's scenario:

2% per year X 30 years= 60%

Average of Highest 2 years X 60%

$71,000 X .60 = $42,600

TM gap: $80,000 -$42,600 = $37,400

What about Dr. Suzanne? Thanks to her use of levers one and two, Suzanne had the smallest **TM gap** to fill. She started teaching right out of college, earned her doctorate, and accrued two additional years of sick leave that she received credit for in retirement. And most impressively, she was able to retire with thirty-three years in the profession at the age of fifty-five! Her **TM gap** was only $10,000 a year.

Dr. Suzanne's scenario with 2 years of sick time accrued:

**33 years worked + 2 years of accrued sick
time = 35**

2% per year X 35 years= 70%

Average of Highest 2 years X 70%

$100,000 X .70 = $70,000

TM gap: $80,000 - $70,000 = $10,000

How much would these teachers have needed to save through paying themselves first to produce between $10,000 and $40,000 dollars a year? How did they save that much?

The answer to this question is that they put their money to work through the miracle of compound interest.

Compound Interest

Compound interest is when you earn interest on the principal investment, and instead of taking the interest out of the investment, you add the interest back into the investment. Then the initial investment grows to be the amount of the principal plus the interest. The new, larger amount then earns interest, which accrues with the new principal. This repeated reinvesting of the interest will grow, much like a snowball. Over time, this snowball of earning interest on your interest grows, and so does your investment. In this manner, your money literally works for you while you sleep.

There's a classic question that's often used to illustrate the power of compound interest in investing: "Which would you rather have:

a million dollars, or a penny on day one that is doubled every day until day thirty?"

Let's think about this for a second. If on day one, you have one penny and it doubles every day, then on day two, you'd have two pennies. If you double those two pennies on day three, you would then have four pennies. On the third day, you'd end up with eight pennies. Maybe a chart would help you see it:

Day 1 = 1 penny	Day 6 = 32 pennies
Day 2 = 2 pennies	Day 7 = 64 pennies
Day 3 = 4 pennies	Day 8 = 128 pennies or $1.28
Day 4 = 8 pennies	Day 9 = 256 pennies or $2.56
Day 5 = 16 pennies	Day 10 = 512 pennies or $5.12

Ok, ok. You've probably had enough of this trend. We're one-third of the way through the month, and we're only at $5.12. There's no way the doubling penny trick (compound interest) would generate more than a million dollars in thirty days! At this point, some people would say, "Give me the million dollars!" Surely, a million dollars is more than you'd have after thirty days of doubling a penny! I mean, the most we could possibly get out of the penny trick is a couple thousand dollars . . . right?

Let's look at the power of compound interest and what happens during the final days of this example:

Day 25 = $167,772.16	Day 28 = $1,342,177.28
Day 26 = $335,544.32	Day 29 = $2,684,354.56
Day 27 = $671,088.64	Day 30 = $5,368,709.12

As you can see, if you chose the million dollars, you would've lost a ton of money! You would've lost, for most people, a lifetime of earnings. Compound interest is so powerful that Albert Einstein referred to it as the eighth wonder of the world.[19] Understanding compound interest and using it in your favor is a major lever if you're going to become a **ME** and eventually become a **TM**.

> ## Compound interest is the eighth wonder of the world.
>
> ### -Albert Einstein

It's important to point out again that this same phenomenon can happen against your favor in the form of debt, specifically consumer debt! When you carry credit debt from month to month, you'll have compound interest working against you instead of for you! You're letting the eighth wonder of the world work for the banks and credit card companies, not you. Do not get into debt, and do not carry credit card debt from month to month! Debt is a wealth killer! I already shared that "there are two types of people: those who understand interest, and those who don't. Those who don't understand it, pay it. Those who do understand it, earn it!" Now that we see the power of compound interest, we have to be the type of people who understand interest! We have to be the type of people who earn it!

We'll need to use compound interest in our favor to produce the income needed to overcome the **TM gap**.

Example #1

Let's look at our friend Doug's scenario. He had a **TM gap** of $37,400 that he needed to fill in order to become a **ME**. That means he needed to have at least $500,000 in an account that averaged 8% a year to produce the $40,000 additional dollars a year. That's a lot easier to get to than the $1,000,000 nest egg of the **TM**.

Using the lever of paying yourself first through budgeting and the magic of compounding interest, Doug could achieve this goal if he began investing $221.20 every month from when he began teaching to when he retired thirty years later. This is assuming he earned 10% interest on his investments during that time period.

Remember that lever three suggested we should budget to pay ourselves first a minimum of 10% of our income. Doug's average income during the last three years of his career was $71,000. A $221.20 investment into an interest-bearing account is well below the minimum suggested investment, yet he still meets his goal of $500,000. Doug still fills the gap between what a **T**rue **M**illionaire receives from their investments and what he will receive from his retirement!

Doug's scenario shows us that a teacher can get into the profession a little later in life, not get any additional degrees, and invest less than 10% of their salary every month during the entirety of his or her thirty-year career, and he or she can still receive the equivalent of what a millionaire would receive from their investments every year of their retirement. Doug can truly become a **M**illionaire **E**quivalent!

It's amazing that Doug could make his goal of becoming a **ME** through his persistent and disciplined leveraging of compound interest over thirty years, but we are left with another question: What would have happened if Doug would have paid himself first the suggested 10% a month?

To illustrate this point and for the sake of simplicity, let's suppose that Doug's average salary throughout his career was $50,000 and that he invested 10% of that income every month for thirty years. That means he would have invested $416.67 every month in an account that earned 10% interest, resulting in him accruing $941,876 in the account. Had Doug followed the counsel to pay himself first a minimum of 10% and to leverage the power of compound interest, he would've ended up close to a True Millionaire in addition to the healthy retirement from his career as a teacher.

Example #2

If you think Doug accomplished his goal easily, wait until you see what our overachieving friend Dr. Suzanne needed to save to overcome the **TM gap**. After all, she only had to produce an additional $10,000 a year.

In order to produce this additional $10,000 a year, Dr. Suzanne would need $125,000 in an account that earns 8% interest every year. That means she would've only needed to start saving a mere $40.47 every month throughout her thirty-three-year teaching career. During the last three years of teaching, Dr. Suzanne averaged $100,000 each year, so $40.47 is far less than the recommended minimum of 10% of her income. Through hard work, discipline, and persistence Dr. Suzanne would easily achieve **ME** status and would more than likely would become a **TM** without any additional effort.

Just for kicks and giggles, let's look at how much Dr. Suzanne would've accrued had she followed the teaching to pay yourself first, and instead of investing a paltry $40 a month, she invested the minimum of 10% of her income. Again, for the sake of simplicity, let's suppose that Dr. Suzanne's average salary throughout her thirty-three-year career was $68,000. That means she would have invested $6,800 a year or an average of $566.66 a month. If she earned an average of 10% interest on these investments over that time, she would have had $1,750,599 in that account alone. Dr. Suzanne would be a **True Millionaire** almost two times over! Keep in mind that this is in addition to her handsome $70,000 a year retirement payout!

So now the question is, how can we put our money to work for us? There are a number of options available to use compound interest for the hard-working, disciplined, and persistent teacher to become a **ME**. The previous examples assumed that the pay-yourself-first funds were invested monthly in an interest-bearing account that earned 10% interest every year.

What retirement accounts are available that earn this percentage of interest consistently? The most common investment opportunity available to teachers is the opportunity to contribute to an employer-offered or personal IRA to supplement the retirement amount the teachers earn and close the **TM gap**. To set up an IRA, there may be options available through your district, you can use an outside vendor, or you can research low cost, no load alternatives that you'd manage on your own. You might consider working with an investment professional to decide which investment products (mutual funds, individual stocks, bonds, etc.) are appropriate for your situation. Like in the chapter before, my purpose is not to advise you on which approach you should take but to explain the basics of each concept and then leave it to you to investigate the options and choose the one that works best for your situation. While an investment professional will help you understand the nuances of each investment option, I will briefly explain the most common options to give you an idea of different options you might look into.

401k vs. 403b

You may see these numbers and letters thrown around quite often, and at first, they might be confusing. Don't worry, you're an educator and you'll get used to acronyms and certain letters and numbers being combined in strange ways. Have you ever heard of an IEP, Title I, or Title IX? We use acronyms all the time in education, just as people do in finance. When you see 401k and 403b, just know that these are simply sections of the IRS tax code that explain the rules that apply to these types of investments. The 401k IRA is a privately held IRA. It can be created by an individual or by an employer in the private sector. Private sector employer's often offer 401ks, and some even match the individual's contributions as part of their benefit package to incentivize participation. The 403b is provided by public sector employer (the government, healthcare organizations, religious organizations, public schools, and non-profit organizations). This option behaves in a similar way to the 401k and will give you similar investment options.

Traditional Plan or Roth Plan

A traditional plan, whether it's a 401k or 403b, is an investment vehicle that takes your money out of your check *before* it's taxed (pre-tax investment). Investment experts will point out that there are two benefits to using a traditional IRA and taking your investment dollars out before it is taxed. The first benefit is that it lowers your taxable income and subsequently will lower your tax burden. The impact of this benefit will vary depending on how much you're contributing each month. If you're only investing $100 a month in this plan, it won't affect the taxes much. But if you're investing $1,500 each month, you may see less taxes taken out of your paycheck. This leads us to the second benefit of pre-tax contributions to a traditional IRA.

Since you would be pulling out money before taxes, potentially lowering the amount of taxes that are taken out of your check, you could conceivably invest more each month. If you planned to pay yourself $100 each month, then you would probably expect to see $100 less in your check. But because the traditional IRA pulls the money out before it is taxed, you might only see a $92 reduction in your check. So if you increased your contribution to $108 each month, you might only see a $100 decrease in your paycheck.

Because you would be putting more money in each month, this could help you use the compound interest on larger amounts every month.

Pre-tax withheld and invested	Actual reduction on paycheck
$100	$92
$108	$100

This sounds good, but there is one drawback. If you're not paying taxes on your contributions every month, when are you paying your taxes on that amount? You may have guessed it; you will pay your taxes when you withdraw your money in retirement. Except, not only would you be paying taxes on all the money that you contributed over the years, but you would also be paying taxes on all that compound interest that the money earned over the years. That's not all; you'd also be taxed at the tax rate you're in at the time of withdrawal. Depending on your situation, you may be in a higher tax bracket when you take these payouts.

A Roth Plan, whether it's a 401k or 403b, is different from the traditional plan in that it pulls your contribution from your check *after* you have paid your taxes. Because you contribute to this fund with after-tax money, when you contribute $100, it lowers your take home pay by $100. You essentially lose the traditional plan's benefit of being able to contribute more each month without seeing your net pay lowered as much.

The benefit of the Roth plan comes when you withdraw your money. Since you've already paid your taxes on the contribution, you don't have to pay taxes when you take the money out of this account. In theory, the account will have benefited from compound interest during the lifetime of the account, and all the growth of a Roth plan is tax-free! Another potential tax advantage of the Roth would be that if you find yourself in a higher tax bracket later in life, you would have already paid taxes on the contribution in a lower tax bracket, meaning you pay less in taxes overall. Yet another benefit of the Roth is that you can withdraw any of your contributions from your account before the age of sixty-five without a penalty or tax burden. This is possible because you've already paid the taxes associated with the contributions since it's an after-tax investment.

While these aren't the only products available for you to use compounding interest to help you close the **TM gap** and become a **ME**, most teachers I know use these two common tools. These tools are readily available and give you even more options for investing such as stocks, mutual funds, money market funds, and fixed annuities.

I suggest researching which option works for your situation, talking to financial professionals, and getting started as soon as you can. The biggest asset you have in investing for the long term is time. Think back to the example of compound interest. The number of pennies doubled *every day*. The investment opportunities we've discussed probably won't double your money every day, but the effect of compound interest is greater the longer you let it grow. If you're early in your career, you can really take advantage of this lever by paying yourself first in the form of 10% monthly contributions to a 401k or 403b, which can help you become a **TM** without too much trouble. If you're further in your career and haven't started to pay yourself first yet, it's never too late to start. As the Chinese proverb says, "The best time to plant a tree was twenty years ago; the second-best time is now."

> **The best time to plant a tree was 20 years ago; the second best time is now**
>
> -Chinese Proverb

On a personal note . . .

I'd read a couple of books on finances in college, so I knew I needed to get into a Roth IRA as soon as possible. It took until January of my first year of teaching to get in a position where I could set an IRA up, and I started contributing $50 a month. My wife started her Roth IRA with the same amount after her first year of teaching. We've consistently contributed throughout our career, but neither of us started by paying ourselves the recommended 10% to 20%. Now I wish we would have invested more, but we wanted to have as much cash available to us in case of an emergency. Over the years, we've increased the percentage of our income that we pay ourselves each month, but we still haven't achieved the aggressive goal of 15% of our income, though we are still committed to get there!

Our funds have behaved much like the first ten days of the compounding interest example. The growth has been slow but steady. Now, after more than twenty years of investing the money that we paid ourselves first, we are starting to see bigger jumps as time passes. It just makes sense that 10% interest on a bigger amount is more than 10% interest on a smaller amount. For example, earning 10% interest on $150,000 produces $15,000, whereas, earning 10% on $10,000 only produced $1,000. As our principal amount grows, so do the jumps in how much we earn through interest. And we haven't even invested for the full thirty years yet. As our kids leave the nest and our earning potential continues to rise, we're planning to pay ourselves 20% of our income for the next seventeen to twenty years, so we still have plenty of time to leverage compound interest in our favor and make us **TM**'s.

Even if you haven't started paying yourself first or investing it for your future, the second best time to plant your money tree is now. There is still time to put your money to work!

The Millionaire and Me

Chapter 5

Lever 5–Expand Your Options

We can see how Doug and Suzanne were able to close the gap between what a True Millionaire's IRA would produce in retirement and what each teacher's full retirement plan would produce each year of their retirement. By paying themselves first and using the power of compound interest through their IRAs, they became a **Millionaire Equivalents**. It might have surprised you that they were able to overcome the **TM gap** so easily. It only took them investing $40 to $220 a month for thirty to thirty-three years to achieve an impressive number. Now that you've closed your own **TM gap** and achieved the status of a **ME**, let's turn our focus to how you can just as easily become a **TM** yourself through investing in your IRA and expanding your options.

In his book *Creating Wealth: Retire in Ten Years Using Allen's Seven Principles of Wealth*, Robert G. Allen names seven wealth principles that are needed to create the wealth we'll discuss in this section. Three of these wealth principles are very much applicable to teachers as they move from a **ME** to a **TM**.

The Millionaire and Me

The first wealth principle is:

Make the maximum use of your assets. Sacrifice to invest in things which go up in value.[20]

I've already mentioned that Robert Kyosaki's definition of an asset is something that puts money into your pocket such as a 401k or 403b. I've also discussed sacrificing to invest in those assets by paying yourself first. We saw that as Doug and Suzanne increased their investment percentage to 10% of their paycheck in the earlier examples, they easily became **MEs**, and Suzanne easily became a **TM**.

I've already referenced the Prodigious Accumulators of Wealth (PAWs) from the book *The Millionaire Next Door* multiple times. Dr. Stanley shared that the average PAW invested 20% of his or her income. What would've happened to the people in our examples if they had sacrificed to invest the full 20% of their incomes? This wealth principle would have allowed them to maximize their assets in their 401k or 403b to become **TMs** many times over. Doug would have taken the value of his investments from **$941,876**, which was earned by investing 10% of his income for thirty years, to **$1,883,754**. Suzanne would have increased the value of her investments from **$1,750,599**, which was earned by investing 10% of her income for thirty years, to **$2,561,855**. Those numbers are astounding!

The trick is to sacrifice each month to invest in things that go up in value. Paying yourself 20% is a sacrifice, but if you invest it, you can easily become a **TM** as we see with Doug and Suzanne.

Lever 5—Expand Your Options

	Investing **10%** earning an average of **10%** interest	Investing **20%** earning an average of **10%** interest
Doug (Investing for 30 years)	$941,876	$1,883,754
Suzanne (Investing for 33 years)	$1,750,599	$2,561,855

The next two wealth principles are likewise easy to apply for teachers:

Wealth seekers are always on the offensive, not on the defensive

Money must multiply at wealth-producing rates of return.[21]

When I created projections for the examples, I purposely made them conservative in nature to show how this is possible. One way to be on the offensive and not on the defensive in investing is finding ways to increase your rates of return on your investments. At this point you're probably wanting to create enough wealth to be a **TM**, so you'll need to find wealth-producing rates of return. The historical rate of return from the S&P 500, which includes the five hundred largest and most stable companies on the New York Stock exchange, shows that people can earn 12% interest a year investing in an S&P 500 fund. From 1923 to 2016, the average rate of return was 12.25%. That span of time included the great depression and the "lost decade" from 2000 to 2009, which included a technology bubble burst, a terrorist attack, and the financial collapse of 2008. This is the reason why the S&P 500 is held as a good reference point for investors.

Let's look at Doug's and Suzanne's numbers if they'd applied all three of these wealth principles and invested 20% of their incomes and earned 12% a year. Doug would have gone from **$1,883,754** to **$2,912,494**. Suzanne would have gone from **$2,561,855** to **$3,960,912**. They both would have earned over a million dollars more just by earning 2% more interest each year!

As you can see, one way to be on the offensive and multiply your money at wealth-producing rates of return is to work with an investing professional to find the best way for you to increase the rates of return on your money.

	Investing **20%** earning an average of **10%** interest	Investing **20%** earning an average of **12%** interest
Doug (Investing for 30 years)	$1,883,754	$2,912,494
Suzanne (Investing for 33 years)	$2,561,855	$3,960,912

I suggest you access a retirement calculator online and play with the numbers. Make a note of how much money you begin with in your account, and adjust the amounts you contribute each month. Then, adjust the percentages you earn each year, personalizing the numbers to match your situation. Doing this can inspire you as you make goals of maximizing your assets, staying on the offense, and making your money multiply at wealth-producing rates.

In *Think and Grow Rich*, Napoleon Hill repeatedly writes about the power of focusing on a goal with intense clarity and continually keeping that goal in mind. He says that the person who has a clear goal and focuses on that goal will achieve his or her goal.[22] I believe in the power of writing goals down and looking at them frequently. You can write your personal money goals in the space provided below to help you have clarity and focus on your goals as you work hard to move from a **ME** to a **TM**.

Amount I have saved for retirement: $_____

Current percentage I'm investing monthly: _____%

Current amount I'm investing monthly: $_____

Goal percentage I want to invest monthly: _____%

Goal amount I want to invest monthly: $_____

Amount I'll have at age 60 if I invest the smaller amount:
$_____

Amount I'll have at age 60 if I invest the larger amount:
$_____

Up until this point, we've only discussed two wealth-building vehicles—your full retirement and your IRA, whether it's a 401k or a 403b. There is another readily available vehicle that many teachers research and invest in to create another stream of income. That vehicle is real estate.

Real estate as a vehicle to wealth

Many financial advisors will encourage you to have real estate as part of your financial portfolio. *The Millionaire Next Door* reports that 97% of the millionaires in the study were homeowners.[23] Owning your home is a worthy goal, but remember that Robert Kyosaki's definition of an asset is something that puts money in your pocket, and a liability is something that takes money out of your pocket.[24] Most people feel that their primary residence is their biggest asset, but in reality, it can be one of their biggest liabilities.

> **An asset is something that puts money in your pocket.**
>
> **- Robert Kyosaki**

This goes counter to how many people think of their homes. In contrast, real estate in the form of rental homes, multiple family units, and commercial real estate could qualify as an asset. If done correctly, these properties consistently put money in your pocket in a variety of ways. If you're trying to move from a **ME** to a **TM**, investment properties are a potential vehicle that can help you get there.

Mutual funds, stocks and other paper assets *generally* will only put money in your pocket in one way—if they go up in value. If the markets go down, then you lose money for that month, quarter or year. Real estate, on the other hand, has multiple ways to put money in your pocket. I will briefly describe four ways real estate can create wealth. For the purposes of our discussion, we will only look at the numbers on a single-family unit as a rental property.

Appreciation

The first source of creating wealth in an investment property is when the value of the property goes up, or appreciates. This typically happens because of market forces in the area—homes that are comparable in the area selling for more, improvements to the property you've done, etc. For example, I bought my first property for $115,000 in the year 2000, and it is valued at $225,000 today.

If I were to sell the property today, I would earn $110,000 or about 3.25% a year in appreciation alone. In some markets, real estate can climb up to 15% a year in appreciation or higher. Other markets are much cooler and earn lower percentages, But the average appreciation in real estate for the country is 3.8%. You may see 3.8% interest and not be very impressed; however, let's not give up on real estate just yet, because there are still three sources of growth in investment real estate that we haven't mentioned.

Cash Flow

Another source of income investment real estate provides is cash flow. If you finance your investment property, the cash flow is the rent collected minus your loan payment. If you collect $1,300 a month in rent and  your payment is $900, then your property creates a cash flow of $400 a month or $4,800 a year. If you don't have a loan on the rental house but own it, all the money that you collect from that house is a positive cash flow. In the case of our example, that would be $1,300 a month or $15,600 a year.

If you put $100,000 in a mutual fund earning 12% a year, it would produce $12,000 a year. If, instead of putting that $100,000 in the mutual fund, you bought a $100,000 house that you rent out for $1,000 a month, the house would generate $12,000 a year. This is in addition to the 3.8% appreciation you'd likely be earning on the property. As you can see, with cash flow and appreciation together, real estate can surpass the mutual fund in how much wealth it generates. And there are still two more ways that this asset puts money in your pocket.

Depreciation and tax incentives

Because real estate is a real asset as opposed to a paper asset (mutual funds, stocks, bonds, etc.), there are tax incentives that exist in this type of investing that don't exist in other markets. The government is interested having housing available for citizens, and it provides tax breaks for people who are willing to take the risk of tying up their capitol in housing. Because of this, you can write off many housing costs from your tax burden such as any losses, insurance payments, or interest payments on loans associated with your investment property. You would need to consult with your tax professional and study these write offs to see how it would affect your situation, but they exist, and, depending on the situation, they can add up to thousands of dollars in savings every year.

Again, these tax write offs are in addition to cash flow and appreciation. These extra goodies do not exist with paper assets.

Another person paying down your loan

If you decide to leverage other people's money (OPM) and finance a property rather than purchase it outright, there is a fourth way real estate puts money in your pocket: someone else (your renter) would be paying your loan payments. Every month someone else pays to live in your property, the amount of the rent that's applied to your principal would lower your principal amount owed and increase your equity in the house. Your renter would essentially be paying your cash flow, taxes, insurance, interest on the loan, and principal. Depending on the terms and maturity of your loan, this could add another $100 to $800 a month that someone else is paying for you. You can then add that principal payment to the amount this asset is putting into your pocket.

Example:

Let's look at an example. Imagine that you didn't have $100,000 cash or that you didn't want use all your money to buy a house, but you did have $20,000 for a down payment. That would mean you would finance the remaining $80,000. Because you have a payment, your cash flow would obviously go down considerably. You would still be collecting $1,000 a month in rental payments, but now you would also be paying your loan payment, which may include principal, interest, taxes, and insurance (PITI), of $800. The money collected for rent will pay down the principal on the loan and still create $200 in monthly cash flow.

When you finance an investment in real estate, you would benefit from the 3.8% appreciation rate, the $200 monthly cash flow, the tax benefits, and, if you finance the house, the benefits of having the renter paying down your loan every month.

Returning to the three wealth-building principles shared earlier in this section (make the maximum use of your assets and sacrifice to invest in things that go up in value; wealth seekers are always on the offensive, not on the defensive; and money must multiply at wealth-producing rates of return), you can see that real estate leverages all three.

It doesn't matter whether you apply the three wealth building principles to your IRAs, to investment real estate, or to another investment tool; in order to become a **TM,** you need to choose the right investments for your situation and make sure those investments increase enough in value to meet your goals. To do that, you will need to make sure you're applying these wealth-building principles consistently.

Maximizing our cash flow.

In *Creating Wealth*, Robert G. Allen said he hated the word retirement because it seemed so final. But just because we retire from teaching, it doesn't mean we're done creating and accumulating wealth that will bless us and our families for decades. Thanks to the retirement plan, we as teachers are able to retire up to a full decade before our peers even think of retiring with a large, stable stream of income coming in every year. Moreover, if we follow the principles outlined in this book, we should retire with very little debt, which means that we should have a good cash flow coming in, and not too much flowing out.

If we want to achieve **TM** status, we can maximize our cash flow by creating more streams of income after we retire. If you get into teaching early, you will be eligible to retire at a relatively young age. Some would argue that such an age would be too early to retire. Luckily, though, you would have time to generate more income well into retirement.

What will your next chapter be? Maybe you would like to reinvent yourself. Maybe you have a business idea. Or maybe you still have some teaching left in the tank and you'd like to get paid more for teaching less.

Double dipping

Many teachers take advantage of yet another benefit that exists in our profession: most states will allow you to draw a full retirement and still work in a part-time capacity, though they generally won't let you work more than half time without it affecting your retirement plan payout. This means you would essentially earn the equivalent of time and a half for working part-time.

I remember when I was working landscaping during college; I had to work more than forty hours in the hot sun just to get to the point of earning time and a half for those hours worked over the forty-hour workweek. In the teaching profession, you can be fifty-five, retired, working part time, and receiving a full retirement without even going out into the sun once! I know many teachers who work part-time after retirement and invest every dollar they make into more assets that will grow and provide additional cash flow when they start to draw from their 401ks and 403bs.

I recently spoke to a friend of mine who did just that. He retired when he was fifty-one years old. In the decade that followed, he found opportunities to work part-time in a few different schools. He invested every penny from his part-time job and lived off his retirement plan payout. At sixty-one years old, he's now sitting on a substantial amount of money. In addition to this benefit, he reminded me that his retirement plan payout increases 3% each year and that now, after ten years of retirement, he's making the same amount from his retirement payout as he was when he was working full time!

I know of other teachers whose children had grown and settled down in another state. They wanted to be closer to their children and grandchildren, so they retired from their state and got a full-time job in the state where their children lived. Could you imagine? You can receive a full retirement payout from your original state and work full-time in another state for three to five years. You could then invest every penny of your income from the new state in assets that would produce income for you and your family for the rest of your life. This would be an additional $300,000 to $500,000 to invest before you're really done working. That would probably be enough to make you a **TM** or at least add to the already impressive amount you've accumulated.

When you follow the principles in this book—you work hard, are disciplined, and persist—the sixty-year-old you will be very happy with the decisions thirty-year-old you made. Heck, the eighty-year-old you will be very happy with the decisions the fifty-five-year-old you made.

This lever can be a little intimidating because it may get us teachers a little out of our comfort zones. Generally, we love kids, our subject expertise, and people, and this lever can feel a little like we're diving into the business and the private sector. However, with hard work, discipline, and persistence, we teachers can really utilize this lever to close the **TM gap** and become **True Millionaires!**

On a personal note . . .

There are a number of ways my wife and I are trying to maximize this lever: (1) We're working to increase how much we pay ourselves first, and we're working with our advisors on how to maximize what our investments are earning. (2) We have made it a point to meet yearly with our investments advisor. We meet at the local

McDonald's, enjoy an egg McMuffin, and discuss any adjustments we can make to our investments. I love a good egg McMuffin, and I love to chat about how we can improve our performance, so it's a real win-win scenario. (3) My wife and I plan on continuing with this practice throughout our retirement to see what we need to do to maximize these assets and to determine how much we need to stay on the offense and how much we need to play defense.

If everything goes as planned, I'll be eligible to retire at the relatively young age of fifty-four and could reasonably work for another five to ten years after that, earning money in addition to my retirement. This means I can do other things to add active income into our investments. In this chapter, we discussed how double dipping could be very profitable, and I hope to find opportunities to double dip. One of my options is to continue teaching at the collegiate level for years to come since it's very enjoyable and is something that I could do in retirement. My wife and I have also discussed looking into other avenues to make additional funds, where we could completely reinvent ourselves. We've discussed possibilities ranging from working at McDonalds to getting my realtor's license and selling houses. Did I mention that I love McDonalds?

When my wife and I first got married, we had good credit and were shocked when the realtor told us we would qualify for a loan that was four times our annual income! At the time, we made a combined $65,000 a year, meaning we could buy a home worth $260,000. In our area, that amount of money would have bought a huge home in a really nice area—much more than we would've needed. We were tempted to look at some bigger homes, but we knew that we did not want to go into that kind of debt. Even though we *could* qualify for that much of a loan, it didn't mean we *should* go into that kind of debt. In the end, we decided to buy a much more sensible home and bought a three-bedroom, two-bath house for $117,000. That amount was less than half of what we qualified for. After two years, we decided that we wanted a few more amenities to better meet the needs of our growing family, and we began to look for another house. Again, our realtor let us know that we could qualify for a much bigger loan than we needed. Instead of getting into too big of a house and its accompanying mortgage, we decided to keep our first home as a rental and bought another reasonable home with only the amenities we wanted. We've been renting out the first home for eighteen years now, and we've seen the house appreciate in value with the market. And our renters have paid down that mortgage considerably.

Because real estate offers so many positives, I later bought another rental with a buddy, and we've managed it for the past sixteen years, splitting the responsibilities and the earnings fifty-fifty.

Our experience with rentals has been mostly positive, but it can be a lot of work when things go wrong. I suggest you research the pros and cons as a family and really learn what you're getting into if you choose to take on this powerful wealth-producing vehicle.

Having said that, the real estate my family owns and manages will be a contributing factor in achieving our goal of closing the **TM gap** and becoming **T**rue **M**illionaires.

Chapter 6

The Law of the Harvest

In this book, we've discussed five levers available to teachers that, if utilized, will bless the lives of you and your family for generations.

The Law of the Harvest

Much has been written of the law of the harvest, which simply says that you reap what you sow, or in other words, you harvest what you plant. Throughout this book, we've discussed the seeds you would need to plant if you want to have the harvest of becoming a millionaire. We've discussed at length the importance of making a goal, creating a plan to achieve that goal, working hard, being disciplined, and persisting to achieve that goal. If we want to harvest apples, we need to plant apple trees. Even if apples and tomatoes look and feel similar, we cannot plant tomatoes and expect to harvest apples. We have to plant the right seeds and nurture those seeds if we want to harvest our goal.

> You reap what you sow. You cannot plant tomatoes and expect to harvest apples.

King Solomon, who is attributed to as the author of Ecclesiastes, wrote, "To every thing there is a season, and a time to every purpose under the heaven: A time to be born, and a time to die; a time to plant, and a time to pluck up that which is planted."[25] When we look at the law of the harvest, there's a planting season, a growing season, and a harvest season and then the harvest gets you through the winter. Farmers obey the laws of nature and use those laws to their advantage. If a farmer violates the laws that pertain to a particular crop, the harvest may suffer or simply may not happen at all. The farmer waters and fertilizes the crops, applies the proper amounts of pesticides and herbicides to make sure that insects don't devour the crop or that the crop doesn't have too much competition from noxious weeds. After the growing season comes the harvest, and the farmers use the best techniques to harvest the crops without damaging them. They time the harvest to allow the crop to mature as much as possible without waiting so long that they lose all the fruits of their labor to an early frost. If the farmer has worked hard, been disciplined, and persisted, there will be ample harvest to cover all the costs that have likely come up throughout the year, that will come up for future crops, and that will come up for the needs of the farm throughout the winter.

Your career is like a harvest. There's a planting season, a growing season, and a harvest season. Then, after harvest, there's a wonderful, magical season where you enjoy the fruits of your labors. We'll call this season *retirement*.

Think of the first ten years of your career as the planting season of your career. During this planting season, you can learn how to become an effective teacher. You may be earning additional degrees and preparing for future opportunities. You can set up a budget and begin to pay yourself first every single month by working with a financial advisor and investing 10% to 20% in something like a 401k or 403b or even an investment home. During this season, you can plant professional and financial seeds that will grow as your career continues. Much like the farmer must follow the laws of nature, you must follow the rules of finance and have faith that these seeds will grow and produce an abundant harvest when needed.

The next ten years of your career can be compared to the growing season. During this growing season, you can continue to finish the next available degree. You develop into a leader and are prepared for more opportunities that potentially have higher salaries. You earn more money and continue to be disciplined and persistent in paying yourself 10% to 20% every month. You meet with your financial advisor every year to determine if any adjustments need to be made to your investments. During this time, your faith in the plan is strengthened as you see the crops growing.

As we carry this analogy to the end, the final ten years of your career would be the harvest. The harvest will see the teacher earning the most money they've made in their career. The degrees and preparation will allow for even more opportunities. Your faith in the  plan transforms into a perfect knowledge, as you're able to harvest enough to be a **ME** and a **TM**. You work with financial advisors to make sure all tax implications are considered to maximize the yield of the harvest.

After the harvest, you can decide what the next chapter of life will be. Will you continue in a part-time capacity? Will you reinvent yourself altogether? There can potentially be years of good health and energy in front of you to double dip to create even more of a harvest for you to enjoy later. You'll have the complete freedom to make whatever choice you want. If, like the farmer, we obey the law of the harvest and treat our careers and our finances like seedlings, then those seedlings will produce a harvest that will meet our needs and the needs of our family for years to come.

I've already shared with you that as a kid, my younger brother and I worked on my grandfather's farm in Southeastern Idaho. It was hard work milking the cow, tending to all of the needs of the farm, and moving the irrigation pipe. As you can imagine, working in a hot potato field for hours on end could get a little boring for a couple teenagers. To spice things up, sometimes one of us would dig out a potato from the row and throw it at the other. This would lead to a full-on potato-throwing war as the other would dig up a potato to return fire. We would have a great time throwing and dodging potatoes before we would have to knock it off and get back to work.

If you pull potatoes out of the ground in June they are small. They are much smaller than the huge Idaho spuds you find in the store. Those were harvested in the fall when they matured. We never told our grandpa of our shenanigans, but I'm sure he wouldn't have appreciated us taking his harvest out of the ground for the short-term gain of entertaining ourselves for a few moments during the tedious and mundane daily routine.

Why do I share this story?

I see many teachers delay getting their extra degrees. I see them not paying themselves first. I see teachers making excuses for not living on a budget. For heavens sakes, I see cars worth more than a teacher's yearly salary parked in school parking lots. I see many teachers turn away opportunities for extra work or positions that will provide growth and extra money. In short, I see teachers do the equivalent of what a couple bored kids did in that potato field; they're pulling their metaphorical spuds out of the ground in June! They're satisfied with a small potato to entertain themselves now rather than letting that potato mature and provide for themselves and their families when harvested at the right time.

Let's not settle for small potatoes! Let's make sure we harvest enormous, huge, delicious, famous Idaho potatoes!

Every one of us will have life hit us; we will have complications to our plans, and we will likely experience boredom in the tedious and monotonous aspects of the career that will tempt us to dig up our potatoes early to do something else. But if we're able to resist those temptations and prepare for the financial buffetings of life, then our harvest will be all the more abundant.

The Hedgehog and the Flywheel

I love two concepts Jim Collins discusses in his book *Good to Great: Why Some Companies Make the Leap . . . And Others Don't.* Collins looked at hundreds of companies that have succeeded over time and studied what made good companies make the leap to great companies while other good companies remained good companies or even ceased to exist. The book identifies two strategies that the companies who made the jump from good to great employed that assisted them in their journey; these strategies are the hedgehog concept and the flywheel effect.

For the hedgehog concept, Collins describes the hedgehog and his foe, the fox. In nature, the fox is sneaky and knows a lot of ways to capture his prey, whereas the hedgehog knows only one defense: it uses a strong muscle in its back to pull itself into a ball. This  causes the sharp spines on its back to stand straight up, thus protecting the soft underbelly. Though the fox is cunning, the hedgehog uses a simple strategy to stay alive and outwit the fox. The hedgehog knows its strengths and weaknesses. When confronted with danger, it does one thing, and it does that thing well until the danger goes away. The fox often gets frustrated or bored because the defense is so effective. Companies that employ this strategy know their strengths and weaknesses and go to their strengths in times of uncertainty. Great companies make a plan, get good at their plan, and stick to that plan even in the face of danger.

The flywheel effect benefits the company in a similar fashion. Collins explained the flywheel effect as follows:

> Picture a huge, heavy flywheel—a massive metal disk mounted horizontally on an axle, about thirty feet in diameter, two feet thick, and weighing about five-thousand pounds. Now imagine that your task is to get the flywheel rotating on the axle as fast and long as possible. Pushing with great effort, you get the flywheel to inch forward,

moving almost imperceptibly at first. You keep pushing and, after two or three hours of persistent effort, you get the flywheel to complete one entire turn. You keep pushing, and the flywheel begins to move a bit faster, and with continued great effort, you move it around a second rotation. You keep pushing in a consistent direction. Three turns . . . four . . . five . . . six . . . the flywheel builds up speed . . . seven . . . eight . . . you keep pushing . . . nine . . . ten . . . it builds momentum . . . eleven . . . twelve . . . moving faster with each turn . . . twenty . . . thirty . . . fifty . . . a hundred.

Then, at some point—breakthrough! The momentum of the thing kicks in in your favor, hurling the flywheel forward, turn after turn . . . whoosh! . . . its own heavy weight working for you. You're pushing no harder than during the first rotation, but the flywheel goes faster and faster. Each turn of the flywheel builds upon work done earlier, compounding your investment of effort. A thousand times faster, then ten thousand, then a hundred thousand. The huge heavy disk flies forward, with almost unstoppable momentum.[26]

Collins points out that great companies kept the focus on their strengths and didn't change directions very often. Companies who struggled would change directions frequently and lose all the momentum they'd already achieved. Often, it took a lot of effort

just to stop the flywheel and then they would need to exert more effort to get the flywheel to start moving in the other direction. When a company works hard, is disciplined, and persists, it gains momentum and the power of compounding interest of investment, and it achieves greatness.

What do the hedgehog and the flywheel have to do with you becoming a millionaire?

As teachers, you have the levers of your maximizing your retirement plan, making the profession pay you, telling your money what to do, putting your money to work, and expanding your options that can all be part of your hedgehog defense. Whenever you begin to doubt what you should do, you simply need to use the strong muscle in your back and curl into a ball and let these five levers stand straight up as your defense. If you're unsure if you should get the extra degree or take a summer school teaching opportunity, use the hedgehog concepts, and take the opportunity. If danger hits your finances and you think you can't pay yourself first this month, use the hedgehog concept and pay yourself first! The hedgehog has faith in its plan, and it always carries out its plan to defend itself. I suggest you do the same.

As teachers, as we consistently maximize the five levers, it will be exactly like pushing on that five-thousand-pound flywheel. Your momentum will be slow at first, but the flywheel *will* move. As you apply the same amount of effort each month, the flywheel of your career will move faster and faster. You don't need to apply more effort—just consistent effort, and the flywheel will consistently gain speed and momentum. If, over time, we maximize our retirements, make the profession pay us by taking opportunities for higher degrees and extra jobs, pay ourselves first, and invest that money consistently, and look for ways to get higher interest on our investments, then we'll leverage the power of compound interest. Doing this will have a flywheel effect on our finances, and it will make us **M**illionaire **E**quivalents and potentially **T**rue **M**illionaires many times over.

None of the concepts discussed in this book are novel, revolutionary, or sexy. You might even think that they're rather common or even boring. Much like in farming, we must participate in an everyday grind to use the laws of finance to our advantage. These levers are tried and true. Anyone in education can use them regardless of his or her circumstances. Simply put, they work!

You can do it!

The Extra Benefits of Teaching

Throughout this book I've shared five specific levers that, if used, will lead to a very good standard of living throughout your career and an excellent standard of living throughout retirement.

I haven't even mentioned other outstanding benefits available to teachers that bring considerable peace of mind. These include insurance options such as health, dental, vision, life, and short-term and long-term care. These benefits are sometimes referred to as the hidden paycheck that you get as an educator.

I haven't mentioned the fact that the work schedule is extremely family friendly. You would be off work when your children are out of school. I don't mean the following as a pejorative, but teachers' contracts are 190 days out of the year. When you think that there are 365 days in a year and your contract is only 190 days, that's pretty awesome.

I haven't mentioned the stability of the profession. I've worked continuously in this profession through one of the biggest economic recessions in this country's history, wartime, and the dotcom bubble burst in addition to the global pandemic of COVID-19. The net effect on the teaching profession during all these economic downturns resulted in a few furlough days at worst and a modest raise at best. And when the economy did well, the raises were better.

What I'm trying to say is that teaching is an excellent profession!

On a personal note . . .

Yes, retiring a millionaire is a great benefit of teaching, but these are not even the best reasons to teach! In the first paragraph of this book, I shared a number of true reasons that make teaching a great profession. Teaching has provided me an opportunity to have an impact on my community in a unique way. The relationships you build with your students as you work with them to learn the content and the real-life lessons that happen in your classroom are transformational. There's no better feeling than running into a current or former student in the

Through the honorable professions of teaching, you can influence individuals, communities and future generations.

community and seeing their eyes light up as you catch up with what they're doing in their lives and reminisce about when they were in your class years before.

My own children have been on the same athletic teams as the children of my former student (that was weird). One time, I was pulled over by a police officer who was a former student. He looked at my driver's license and incredulously asked, "Señor Frandsen?" Let me just say it was quite an emotional swing going from the frustration and nerves associated with getting pulled over to the excitement and pure joy of getting reacquainted with a former student. I will neither confirm nor deny whether I received a traffic citation that day. When my fifth child was born prematurely with life-threatening health issues, he was transported by ambulance to a specialized hospital downtown to treat him. The social worker who received me at the hospital to support my family and me during this family crisis was a former student. During my career, I've seen former students develop into incredible professionals, parents, and community members. Some have even become teachers and school counselors themselves.

I share these stories because the teaching career really does have it all. Through the honorable profession of teaching, you can influence individuals, communities, and future generations. These are the real reasons why we persist in teaching, and the fact that we can become a millionaire in the process is just icing on the cake.

The Millionaire and Me

Acknowledgements

I would like to thank all of those who participated in this project: Aubrey Parry at ravishingingrevisions@gmail.com for your insightful and fearless feedback and editing skills, Laura Knudsen and Zabe Human for your realistic perspective, Nathan Pinnock for your encouragement and insights, Ty Frandsen for your mad illustration skills, Lori Jackson for showing me the way to self-publish a book, my extended family for your encouraging comments throughout the process, my kids for your excitement and occasional teasing about "the book," and especially my son Brian for your crazy talent in figuring out how to put a book cover together.

And finally, I would like to thank my wife, Ashley, for encouraging me to take the kids to practice with the enticement that "[I] could get some writing time on [my] book" and for allowing me to neglect some household responsibilities during this project. You truly are the best!

Notes

1. Thomas J. Stanley, PhD and William D Danko, PhD, *The Millionaire Next Door: The Surprising Secrets of America's Wealthy* (Longstreet Press, 1996), 9.

2. Chris Hogan, *Everyday Millionaires: How Ordinary People Built Extraordinary Wealth – and How You Can Too* (Ramsey Press, 2019).

3. Madeline Will, "5 Things to Know About Today's Teaching Force," in *Edweek.org*.

4. Stephen R. Covey, *Seven Habits of Highly Effective People: Powerful Lessons in Personal Change* (First Free Press, 1989), 95–145.

5. Richard T. Kyosaki, *Rich Dad Poor Dad: What the Rich Teach Their Kids About Money – That The Poor And Middle Class Do Not* (Plata Publishing, 1997), 46.

6. Will, "5 Things to Know."

7. "Teacher Retirement System of Georgia Member's Guide" (2021). https://www.trsga.com/wp-content/uploads/Members-Guide-with-Cover.pdf.

8. "Gwinnett County Teachers Salary Schedule" (2020).

9. Napoleon Hill, *Think and Grow Rich* (The Ralston Society, 1937), 42.

10. Rory Vaden, *Take the Stairs: 7 steps to Achieving True Success* (New York: Penguin Group, 2012), 8.

11. George S. Clason, *The Richest Man in Babylon* (New York: Penguin Books, 1955), 24.

12. Dave Ramsey, *The Total Money Makeover: A Proven Plan for Financial Fitness* (Nelson Books, 2013), 94.

13. Stanley and Danko, *The Millionaire Next Door*, 10.

14. David Bach, *The Automatic Millionaire: A Powerful One-Step Plan to Live and Finish Rich* (New York: Crown Publishing Group, 2016), 10.

15. Mark Victor Hansen and Robert G. Allen, *The One Minute Millionaire: The Enlightened Way to Wealth* (New York: Harmony Books, 2002), 238–242.

16. Elizabeth Warren, *All Your Worth: The Ultimate Lifetime Money Plan* (First Free Press, 2005), p. 14.

17. Dave Ramsey, *Financial Peace Revisited* (New York: Viking Press, 2003), 90.

18. "Understanding Credit Card Interest" in *Investopedia.com* (2021).

19. Jim Schleckser, "Why Einstein Considered Compound Interest the Most Powerful Force in the Universe," in *Inc.com* (2020).

Notes

20. Robert G. Allen, *Creating Wealth: Retire in Ten Years Using Allen's Seven Principles of Wealth* (New York: Simon Schuster, 1986), 33–46.

21. Allen, *Creating Wealth*, 33–46.

22. Hill, *Think and Grow Rich*, 293.

23. Stanley and Danko, *The Millionaire Next Door*, 9.

24. Kyosaki, *Rich Dad Poor Dad*, 46.

25. *The Holy Bible* (KJV), Ecclesiastes 3:1–8.

26. Jim Collins, *Good to Great: Why Some Companies Make the Leap . . . And Others Don't* (New York: Harper Business, 2001), 99, 174–175.

About the Author

Dr. Steve Frandsen's career in education has spanned three decades. Throughout his career, he has held many positions in a large urban school district in the Southeastern United States. He has worked as a high school teacher for Spanish and English as a Second Language, an assistant principal at the elementary and middle school levels, and a principal at the elementary and high school levels. He has also been an adjunct college professor teaching graduate courses in education for the past fourteen years.

Currently, Dr. Frandsen is working as the principal of an alternative high school and is an adjunct professor in the College of Education where he teaches courses for teachers earning advanced degrees in education.

Beyond working with teachers to improve the lives of kids, he has made it a practice to point out the incredibly positive aspects of the teaching compensation package to teachers and potential teachers. For the past decade, he has counseled new and veteran teachers about the power of their retirement plan, encouraged teachers to increase their earning potential through education, and taught them of the need to supplement their retirement through a consistent investment strategy. The reaction to these conversations inspired him to share these concepts with a larger audience through this book.

Dr. Frandsen holds degrees in education from Brigham Young University, Brigham Young University-Idaho, Piedmont College, and Nova Southeastern University. He also earned his Leadership Add-On Credentials from the University of Georgia. Apart from spending time teaching and learning, he loves spending time with his wife and his five children.

If you would like to reach Dr. Frandsen you may contact him at millionaireandme@gmail.com.

Did you enjoy the book?

Share on your social media and order a copy
for a teacher you know!

www.amazon.com/dp/B091F3JFD5/

Made in United States
Orlando, FL
31 May 2024

47367945R00075